Conflict and Connection

The goals of Boynton/Cook's Young Adult Literature series are twofold: to present new perspectives on young adult literature and its importance to the English language arts curriculum and to offer provocative discussions of issues and ideas that transcend the world of the adolescent to encompass universal concerns about the search for identity, security, and a place in life. The contributing authors are leading teachers and scholars who have worked extensively with adolescents and are well read in the genre. Each book is unique in focus and style; together, they are an invaluable resource for anyone who reads, teaches, and/or studies young adult literature.

Titles in the Series

Conflict and Connection

The Psychology of Young Adult Literature

Sharon A. Stringer

Boynton/Cook Publishers
HEINEMANN
Portsmouth, NH

Boynton/Cook Publishers, Inc.
A subsidiary of Reed Elsevier Inc.
361 Hanover Street
Portsmouth, NH 03801–3912

Offices and agents throughout the world

Library of Congress Cataloging-in-Publication Data
Stringer, Sharon A.
    Conflict and connection : the psychology of young adult literature
/ Sharon Stringer.
       p.   cm. — (Young adult literature)
    Includes bibliographical references.
    ISBN 0-86709-415-X
    1. Young adult literature—History and criticism. 2. Adolescence
in literature. 3. Adolescent psychology. I. Title. II. Series:
Young adult literature series (Portsmouth, N.H.)
PN1009.A1S85   1997
809'.89283—dc21   97–3489
                                                     CIP

Consulting editor: Virginia R. Monseau
Production: Vicki Kasabian
Cover design: Jenny Jensen Greenleaf
Manufacturing: Louise Richardson

Printed in the United States of America on acid-free paper
01 00 99 98 97 DA 1 2 3 4 5

To my family, with love

Contents

Contents

Acknowledgments

I want to express my deep appreciation to Virginia Monseau, who encouraged me during every phase of this project. She answered numerous questions, read prior drafts, and provided invaluable feedback and guidance to me. Special gratitude also goes to Peter Stillman and the staff of Heinemann-Boynton/Cook. I am also very grateful to Youngstown State University for awarding me a sabbatical during 1995–1996 so that I could work full time on the book. By example and through sharing, my brother John and my sister Peggy opened up my eyes to new understanding. My friend Libby Vernon and her family continue to be a source of inspiration and love for me. My godchild, Kate du Bray, and I discussed several young adult novels during our visits. Together, we composed one of the paragraphs in Chapter 6. Meg du Bray offered her sunshine and creative insights as well. The Beat Coffee House supplied many nourishing breaks. The interchange of ideas with teachers in Youngstown was a seminal part of the book and a definite source of enjoyment. Very special appreciation and thanks also go to my family and to the following people: John Gard, Maryann Porosky, Richard Petruce, Gary Lloyd, Suzanne Reid, Mamie Smith, Joan Guty, Jim Garland, Joyce Allison, Barry Peterson, Paula Nasci, Mary Ann Kessler, and to my friends and colleagues in the Psychology department and English department at Youngstown State University.

Preface

If I only knew then what I know now. How often have we heard or said this? Conflict and change can create wisdom yet are especially painful, awkward aspects of the adolescent passage. The purpose of *Conflict and Connection: The Psychology of Young Adult Literature* is to help teachers, parents, and teenagers better understand themselves by examining young adult fiction in the context of adolescent psychology. The struggles of adolescence are universal. Discovering who we are, developing autonomy, facing conflict, establishing intimacy, and resisting peer pressure are lifelong tasks. How we deal with these issues during adolescence influences our adulthood. Some people work harder and resolve these issues more than others. The resolution is never final but has important impact on our subsequent relationships. Educators, parents, and others are more effective with youth when they address these central issues in their own lives on an ongoing basis.

This text also explores the universal themes of adolescence through young adult literature and psychological studies in order to counteract our culture's ambiguity and negative stereotypes about teenagers. The timeless themes offer stability and durability. Both disciplines are relatively new, explore similar dilemmas, and offer fertile ground for innovative teaching methods. Discussing universal themes offers insight to people who are attempting to sort through cultural myths about adolescence.

Young adult literature raises powerful ethical dilemmas. Young adult fiction includes topics such as gang violence, drug addiction, homosexuality, suicide, and sexual abuse. These themes can open wounds and awaken many complex emotions in adults as well as adolescents. We often feel unprepared to deal with these important sensitive topics, no matter what age we are. Literature provides objectivity. Because individuals are reading about someone else who is struggling, they may feel more comfortable talking about these issues. *Conflict and Connection: The Psychology of Young Adult Literature* discusses the themes of young adult fiction in the context of information about normal development and signs of risk during adolescence. This

assist teachers in the classroom when they discuss
pressure, and adolescents' risk taking in novels such
e's *The Contender* (1967) and Sue Ellen Bridgers' *Per-*
ns (1987).

observe that during early adolescence, young people
lack-and-white thinking can lead them to premature
ieving that "nothing bad can happen to me," and
tands me," teenagers may view their circumstances
oneliness or depression as permanent (Elkind 1984,
994, 45–73). Some adolescents hold romantic con-
a factor linked to suicide in psychology and young
(Dacey and Kenny 1994, 375; Arrick 1980, 79). These

qualities increase young people's difficulties.

Young adult literature provides valuable information about intervention and prevention of adolescents' problems. For example, Richard Peck's *Remembering the Good Times* (1985) and Fran Arrick's *Tunnel Vision* (1980) offer knowledge about the warning signs of suicide. Similarly, readers gain valuable information about sexual abuse or parental alcoholism in novels such as Chris Crutcher's *Chinese Handcuffs* (1989), Hadley Irwin's *Abby, My Love* (1985), and Alden Carter's *Up Country* (1989). Judith Guest's *Ordinary People* (1976), Hannah Green's *I Never Promised You a Rose Garden* (1964), and Zibby Oneal's *The Language of Goldfish* (1980) inform us about the steps of recovery. Novels such as *The Language of Goldfish*, *Ordinary People*, and *Up Country* sensitively portray how individuals benefit from open communication and counseling.

Similarly, knowledge of adolescents' social and emotional development is valuable for teachers when they discuss fear of homosexuality and peer pressure in Bette Greene's *The Drowning of Stephan Jones* (1991). It is not uncommon for young people to wonder at some time whether they are homosexual. At this time, males and females also tend to be more rigid in their perspectives of masculinity and femininity and behave along more traditional, stereotypical lines (Steinberg and Levine 1990, 99, 177, 182). These findings may help us understand why victimization, intimidation, and codes of silence develop in peer cultures.

Illuminating constructive coping methods in the psychology of young adult fiction offers additional preparation for teachers, parents, and adolescents. These strategies connect to Lazarus' description of "problem-focused" coping as explained by Dacey and Kenny (1994,

356). "Problem-focused" coping includes planning steps and generating diverse solutions in order to cope with stressful situations and problems. Exploring adolescent psychology through young adult literature provides another constructive avenue for individuals to develop "problem-focused" coping techniques. Both young adult literature and psychological studies demonstrate how people develop resiliency despite fear, cultural intolerance, or hardship. Ongoing comparisons of problem solving in literature and psychology are important because expertise changes and there are many different schools of thought.

In a recent 1996 issue of the *Journal of Research on Adolescence*, researchers describe how often the findings of psychological studies are inaccessible to people in the community. As one investigator describes,

> Little scientific knowledge on adolescent development reaches non-scholars such as parents, practitioners, and local policymakers who could benefit from it. . . .
>
> Very few researchers make an effort to translate and disseminate their research to audiences outside of academia, leading to most empirical social science knowledge never reaching the many audiences who might benefit from it. It simply sits on a shelf buried within the pages of a journal. (Small, 11–12)

Fortunately academicians, practitioners, and others are collaborating across institutions in order to address this gap.

This book offers another collaborative link. Examining young adult literature through the lens of adolescent psychology facilitates communication among academic researchers, teachers, parents, and teenagers in the community. Breaking new ground, it offers the best of both worlds by stirring our emotions and enhancing psychological understanding.

A major theme throughout this book is the connection between our inner and outer world. Our view of both influences how well we respond to developmental challenges. Each chapter includes examples from young adult fiction and psychological studies of how individuals can achieve self-determination. I also explore factors that potentially limit our inner and outer world.

Chapter 1, "Who Am I?" illustrates the identity conflicts of male and female protagonists in several novels of Robert Cormier, Cynthia Voigt, Sue Ellen Bridgers, and others. In the analyses of young adult fiction, I discuss the concepts of Erik Erikson, James Marcia, and others. Examples from young adult literature of concepts such as the moratorium, fidelity, and positive self-esteem highlight several internal changes that accompany identity achievement and self-understanding.

Chapter 2, "Home, Where I Grow Up," explores family relationships in the novels of Bill and Vera Cleaver, Zibby Oneal, and others.

I link the orphans of young adult literature to psychologists' descriptions of how adolescents separate from families. This chapter also examines emotional autonomy, parent-adolescent conflict, and parenting styles of discipline. These topics clarify how people develop self-reliance and intimacy. During the process of change, parents may see mirror images of themselves in their children. These themes add richness to our appreciation of "character development" and "coming of age" in both literature and life.

Chapter 3, "Friends Through Thick and Thin," looks at the positive and negative influence of peer groups on teenagers' development. I examine reciprocity and self-disclosure in friendships, intimidation, and popularity. Probing these topics in young adult fiction and psychological studies can help teachers and students to develop realistic concepts of heroism, conformity, intimidation, and intimacy.

In Chapter 4, "There's a War Going on Inside My Head," I decipher protagonists' internal conflicts in novels such as Robert Cormier's *I Am the Cheese* (1977), and Avi's *The True Confessions of Charlotte Doyle* (1990). I refer to the work of Jean Piaget and David Elkind in order to describe aspects of early and late formal operational thinking, adolescents' increased self-awareness, and teens' egocentrism. These topics provide teachers with a variety of tools for challenging the cognitive skills of their students.

Chapter 5, "Finding My Niche," delves into topics such as artistic achievement, intelligence, competition, success, and failure in young adult literature and psychological studies. By studying such themes, teachers can foster critical thinking among students as they compare the decision making skills of protagonists.

What catalyzes moral development? In Chapter 6, "Right from Wrong: I Wish I Knew What to Do," I analyze the ethical dilemmas of parents, teachers, and adolescents in young adult fiction such as Robert Cormier's *After the First Death* (1979) and *The Chocolate War* (1974). I discuss the work of Lawrence Kohlberg, Carol Gilligan, and Harriet Lerner. This analysis illuminates examples of moral courage in literature and life as people develop internal criteria and subjectivity in their judgments of right and wrong.

The central focus of Chapter 7, "My Sexuality: Fantasy Versus Reality," is to explore the impact of adolescent sexuality on different aspects of identity development, morality, and peer relationships. In this chapter, I review topics such as cultural myths of beauty, the connection between physical and psychological well-being, and romantic relationships in young adult literature.

Chapter 8, "I Must Be Going Crazy," focuses upon the problems of adolescence such as alienation, suicide, and emotional illness. I examine themes such as risk, survival, and recovery in young adult literature and psychological studies. Fine tuning our understanding of the connection between illness and health reduces black-and-white thinking about abnormal and normal development. Young adult fiction and psychology both illustrate how problems can be important sources of growth and achievement.

Works Cited

Arrick, F. 1980. *Tunnel Vision*. Scarsdale, NY: Bradbury Press.

Avi. 1990. *The True Confessions of Charlotte Doyle*. New York: Avon.

Bridgers, S. E. 1987. *Permanent Connections*. New York: HarperKeypoint.

Carter, A. R. 1989. *Up Country*. New York: Scholastic.

Cormier, R. 1974. *The Chocolate War*. New York: Dell.

————. 1977. *I Am the Cheese*. New York: Dell.

————. 1979. *After the First Death*. New York: Dell.

Crutcher, C. 1989. *Chinese Handcuffs*. New York: Dell.

Dacey, J., and M. Kenny. 1994. *Adolescent Development*. Madison, WI: WCB Brown & Benchmark.

Elkind, D. 1984. *All Grown Up and No Place to Go: Teenagers in Crisis*. Reading, MA: Addison-Wesley.

Green, H. 1964. *I Never Promised You a Rose Garden*. New York: The New American Library.

Greene, B. 1991. *The Drowning of Stephan Jones*. New York: Bantam Books.

Guest, J. 1976. *Ordinary People*. New York: Ballantine Books.

Hadley, L., and A. Irwin. 1985. *Abby, My Love*. New York: Atheneum.

Lipsyte, R. 1967. *The Contender*. New York: HarperCollins.

Oneal, Z. 1980. *The Language of Goldfish*. New York: Penguin Books USA.

Peck, R. 1985. *Remembering the Good Times*. New York: Dell.

Pipher, M. 1994. *Reviving Ophelia: Saving the Selves of Adolescent Girls*. New York: Ballantine Books.

Small, S. 1996. "Collaborative, Community-Based Research on Adolescents: Using Research for Community Change." *Journal of Research on Adolescence* 6(1): 9–22.

Steinberg, L., and A. Levine. 1990. *You and Your Adolescent: A Parent's Guide for Ages Ten to Twenty*. New York: Harper & Row.

One

Who Am I?

There may be a lone ranger, a drifter, a clinging vine, or an anxious explorer inside each of us. We discover answers to the complex question "Who am I?" by experimenting, inquiring, and committing ourselves to choices. The generally accepted conceptualization of identity achievement in psychology is reflected in the question "Who am I?". It is intricately tied to our self-understanding. Both identity achievement and self-understanding evolve continuously throughout life and enhance people's ability to reach their full potential. Self-understanding intrigues some of us because we believe it enhances our well-being. Yet, we may also avoid self-knowledge because it can raise new, disturbing questions. At times, we prefer acting rather than analyzing ourselves in minute detail. Identity achievement and self-understanding provide the psychological freedom that enables us to balance self-reflection with realistic action.

As teachers, we hope to promote identity achievement, stimulate in-depth change, and nurture internal feelings of self-worth in ourselves and our students without taking shortcuts or promoting superficial change. We may wonder what identity achievement and self-understanding look like on the outside, but we know it stems from the inside, too. Combining the strong characterization of protagonists in young adult literature with concepts in adolescent psychology features the internal changes behind identity achievement. These inner transformations influence behaviors and vice versa.

Society's Children

As Erik Erikson and other psychologists stress, cultural factors explain why identity development is complex and requires ongoing evaluation. Society offers very complex values and definitions of morality

1

and psychological health. As a result, individuals' ability to make sound ethical choices, to refuse roles that do not fit, and to discover strength for the future is difficult. Also, society presents mixed, ambiguous messages about adolescence. Psychologist David Elkind (1981) cautions about the hazards of this "hurried generation" of young people who are pressured to grow up too soon (3–22). Yet, researchers also view adolescence as a protracted stage of development because teenagers need more training and education before they can attain meaningful roles or jobs (Fuhrmann 1990, 68).

There is much pressure on young people today as they face simultaneous changes. In *Reviving Ophelia: Saving the Selves of Adolescent Girls*, Mary Pipher (1994) describes how our society threatens adolescent girls' authenticity and soulfulness just as they face multiple demands at key transition periods (37). She points out that adolescents may lose connection with their true self because of cultural values. Conflicting messages about what is socially acceptable come from family, peer groups, and other sources. This friction heightens teenagers' vulnerabilities.

Surviving the Extraordinary: The Doggie Paddle

Both psychological studies and young adult literature offer examples of how identity can evolve through adolescents' struggle to survive extraordinary circumstances. Life and death experiences can strip individuals of pretense. These close calls enable people to redefine their self-concepts, shift priorities, and reduce senseless violence or conflict.

For example, Susan Hinton's novel *The Outsiders* (1967) illustrates how young people struggle to survive gang warfare, value friendships, strengthen bonds, cope with parental hostility, and reassess their priorities. In this novel, brothers and other young men cope with rivalry, tension, and violence that escalates between two gangs, the Socs and the Greasers. Several gang members die. The protagonist, Ponyboy, and his brothers reaffirm their love for each other and see how destructive violence is. They decide to stop fighting among themselves. Ponyboy becomes more determined to tell his story about life on the streets in order to help other teens and to improve the quality of his life.

Another young adult novel, Ivy Ruckman's *No Way Out* (1988), also illustrates how surviving adversity influences identity development. A group of young people begin a carefree hiking trip along a river. Their trek turns into a terrifying ordeal when a storm occurs and traps them near high flood waters. Fighting to survive, the female protagonist, Amy, reassesses her relationships, recognizes others' courage, takes fewer things for granted, and grows in personal strength.

In literature and life, adolescents cope with additional crises such as parents' psychological abandonment, loss through death, disillusionment, defeat, exposure, and resistance to corruption or to intimidation. These stressful experiences may swallow some individuals and stimulate identity achievement in others. In response to significant stress, adolescents choose different paths of identity achievement that foster resiliency or vulnerability.

Surviving the Ordinary

Identity development also evolves as the person makes daily decisions about what to wear, whom to talk to, what music to listen to, and what social activities to choose. Although these decisions may seem minor, they also influence a person's identity development (Marcia 1980, 160–161).

Moreover, surviving extraordinary circumstances can enable people to find fullfillment in ordinary events. One remarkable adolescent who develops this appreciation during extreme adversity is Anne Frank. Her diary, *The Diary of A Young Girl* (1995), written between 1942 and 1944, describes how she and her family survive while hiding from the Nazis in a secret annex. Anne writes about the ordeals and ordinary moments of people living in cramped, deprived conditions. Looking outside at the sky, fighting monotony, enjoying birthday celebrations, weathering family squabbles, kissing a young man named Peter, and knowing tremendous fear are some of the experiences she describes. These events influence her daily life and her identity development. Anne transforms herself by illuminating the ordinary and extraordinary aspects of her situation.

What Psychologists Say About Identity

In his book *Identity: Youth and Crisis*, Erik Erikson (1968) describes an eight-stage model of psychosocial development (91–141). At any stage, psychosocial conflicts are not resolved in dichotomous fashion but instead involve the integration of two opposing tensions. Erikson highlights identity development as the central challenge for adolescents who are at the fifth stage of psychosocial development, but he does not propose that identity formation is completely resolved at this stage. Erikson and others often depict identity formation as an ongoing process (Atwater 1992, 233; Marcia 1994, 68; Steinberg 1983, 266–268).

James Marcia (1994) extends Erikson's study of identity achievement (67–80). He describes four major identity statuses— *identity diffusion, identity foreclosure, moratorium,* and *achievement* based on two key dimensions of exploration and commitment. Exploration involves examining different options, whereas commitment refers to a person's firm choice for continuous effort in areas such as career, education, and religion.

I Cannot Make a Commitment

Identity confusion is relatively common during early adolescence (Muuss 1988, 68; Rice 1996, 197). It is also referred to as identity diffusion. A person who is identity-confused has not experienced crises and lacks commitment and purpose. Without a core set of values or sense of self, identity-confused youth are aimless, bitter, or apathetic. Identity confusion is expressed in diverse ways during adolescence. The young person who is mesmerized by fads, is lost in the crowd, uses drugs, or engages in delinquency illustrates identity confusion. Individuals also express identity confusion through isolation, disillusionment, and alienation. More serious adjustment problems evolve when young people develop a lifelong pattern of identity confusion (Muuss 1988, 68). The person's inner confusion and apathy is mirrored in his or her outer life as well.

Examples of teenagers' temporary and permanent identity confusion exist in young adult fiction. In Chris Crutcher's novel *Running Loose* (1983), the protagonist, Louie, is confused about his identity after his girlfriend Becky's death. Distant, uninvolved in school, he fights authority and disrupts Becky's funeral. Louie resolves his confusion, however, as he focuses on realistic hurdles and builds connections to others. He works temporarily on a job with his father. The work offers valuable time for Louie to sort through his feelings. With a coach's guidance, he also begins to train for running track in competition.

Robert Cormier's novel *I Am the Cheese* (1977) illustrates how psychological warfare can lead to identity confusion. In this story, the protagonist, Adam Farmer, begins a dangerous journey in search of his parents who disappeared after his father provided secret testimony to a special Senate committee. His father's testimony incriminated other people. A doctor interviews Adam about his past in order to locate his missing parents. Adam carefully weighs the risks of disclosing too much when he answers the doctor's questions because he is not sure whom to trust. Slowly, he integrates information about his past and ultimately recalls how his parents died. Whether Adam is emotionally ill, has memory loss from trauma, or is a pawn in a deadly chase by criminals is an ongoing question. At the end of this novel, Adam rides his bicycle at a hospital, greeting other patients. He may be in a permanent state of identity confusion, a victim of other's duplicity.

Tell Me Who I Should Be

James Marcia and others describe identity foreclosure as a less-mature identity status that can occur often during junior high school through conformity to peers (Muuss 1988, 71). Individuals who are identity-foreclosed choose a job, adopt fads, or follow values without experimentation. Their choice is based on the preferences of peers, parents, teachers, or others. They select an identity prematurely, avoiding experimentation and conflict. By closing options, identity foreclosure constricts people's inner and outer world. Individuals with this identity status might avoid people who raise questions such as "Is this what you really want to do with your life?"; "Have you considered other options?"; "Are you doing this simply to please other people?"; or "What are the pros and cons of making this choice?" These questions may be too threatening if they raise doubts in a person's mind.

One of the main characters in Robert Cormier's *After the First Death* (1979) illustrates identity foreclosure. In this story, terrorists hold children as hostages on a bus. Kate, the bus driver, is trying to escape the terrorists and save the children. Miro, one of the terrorists, obeys a commander named Artkin with unwavering loyalty. When he does not question his allegiance to Artkin, Miro demonstrates identity foreclosure. However, Kate begins to penetrate the cracks in his armor. She asks Miro about his past and tries to get him to think about what he is doing. Through Kate's probing, Miro occasionally falters or shows lapses in attention. Kate uses these slips to try to escape the terrorists. However, Artkin distorts the truth, uses propaganda, and reprimands Miro whenever he slips from total obedience.

I'm Going to Do Just the Opposite

Erikson (1968) also describes negative identity as an unhealthy alternative to identity achievement (172–176). The person who selects a negative identity deliberately chooses a role or set of values that are against parents' standards and society's norms. A negative identity may be a temporary expression of rebellion against a society or family who have not offered worthwhile roles to young people. Minority youth and adolescents from privileged backgrounds may commit crimes, drop out of school, and rebel against all authority (Dacey and Kenny 1994, 185–186; Steinberg 1983, 272). Erikson does not view negative identity as a healthy solution to the identity crisis. He also observes the danger of a young person permanently adopting a negative identity if adults, peers, or other authority figures expect nothing from this person.

Hinton's novel *The Outsiders* (1967) provides a timeless example of how young people who cannot enter mainstream society are forced to choose a negative identity. Some members of the Greasers gang select a negative identity and engage in criminal activities. The community views them as deviant outsiders. They have conflict with another gang, the Socs, who terrorize and victimize the Greasers.

Hinton's novel also illustrates how deviancy and championship exist in the eye of the beholder; society's labels for youth can fluctuate. People in the community view the Greasers as marginal members of society, judging most of the boys by their outward appearance. Yet, one gang member demonstrates much heroism by saving the lives of young children who were trapped in a fire. After the successful rescue, newspapers describe several boys as heroes. Young people need opportunities for positive, useful roles and recognition in their culture.

Ponyboy, the protagonist, voices his own concern about the damage of society's quick judgments of young people who live on the fringe of society. After gang members die, he wishes to prevent other teens from adopting a life of crime. He says:

> I could see boys going down under street lights because they were mean and tough and hated the world, and it was too late to tell them that there was still good in it, and they wouldn't believe you if you did. It was too vast a problem to be just a personal thing. There should be some help, someone should tell them before it was too late. Someone should tell their side of the story, and maybe people would understand then and wouldn't be so quick to judge a boy by the amount of hair oil he wore. (155)

Our culture changes so rapidly that people may become desensitized to the increased violence. Today, if individuals choose a negative identity, they may have to adopt more extreme behaviors in order to be labeled marginal, because of the proliferation of violence in society.

I'm Experimenting

Erikson (1968) and Marcia (1994) propose that in order to achieve identity, individuals experiment with different roles, values, beliefs, and fads before choosing a career, religion, or political ideology. This experimentation is labeled the moratorium. Erikson views the moratorium as a time of exploration (157), and Marcia describes it as one of four possible identity statuses (74–75). During the moratorium, people question and reevaluate their beliefs, values, or career choices. It can occur in college when individuals meet diverse people and experience new events. As they experiment, individuals may feel anxious (Rice 1996, 198–199). However, their constructive search eventually enables them to form a healthier, sturdier identity.

Often, the moratorium occurs as a journey in young adult fiction. In Cynthia Voigt's *Homecoming* (1981), four Tillerman children are homeless after their mother abandons them in a parking lot. They begin a long journey in search of their mother. While staying at their Cousin Eunice's house, the Tillerman children are informed by the police that their mother is in a mental hospital and is very ill. At Cousin Eunice's, they try to adapt and fit a particular lifestyle. Yet, some of the children seem spiritless. One of the boys, Sammy, has fights at school. Dicey, the oldest, believes that adults are mislabeling her sister, Maybeth, as disabled. Something important is missing at Cousin Eunice's home, so the Tillermans eventually decide to leave.

The children's endurance enables them to eventually develop a home with their grandmother. This decision to stay with her is based on a firm conviction that they can survive on their own if necessary. As the children travel, they learn how to stay together, to stop hiding their talents or lose their spunk just to be obedient at home or to be popular at school. The children sail on a boat during their journey. In Voigt's sequel, *Dicey's Song* (1982), Dicey scrapes old paint off a boat in the barn at her grandmother's house as well. The boat is a symbol of self-direction, movement, and change. Through experimentation, the Tillermans find answers to questions about their identities.

Adolescents and their parents may perceive the necessity for the search differently. In Paul Zindel's *The Pigman* (1968), John, a high school sophomore, explains to his father that he needs time to discover who he is. His father does not see John's roadblocks. In the following conversation, John and his father exchange different views:

> "Oh Dad, can't you see all I want to do is be individualistic?"
> "Don't worry about that."
> "I want to be me."
> "Who's asking you not to be?"
> "You are."
> "I am not. I don't want you to go along with the crowd. I want you to be your own man. Stand out in your own way."
> "You do?"
> "Of course I do . . ."
> "Just give me a little longer to find out who I am . . ." (60).

Other novels describe adolescents' journeys to contact a parent who has disappeared. Young adult literature includes many stories of parents who left home. For some protagonists, parental absence triggers an identity search and separation from family. Until they reconnect to this missing parent, orphans may feel as if an important part of themselves is buried. In Bruce Brooks' *Midnight Hour Encores* (1996) and Jean Thesman's *The Rain Catchers* (1991), daughters decide to visit their mothers who live away from home. As they travel and visit their mothers, the young women temporarily modify their current lifestyles and explore new values, clothing, and activities. Through experimentation, these young women make important discoveries about themselves. Returning home, they feel a renewed sense of wholeness. In *The Rain Catchers*, (1991) the female protagonist, Grayling, develops a deeper appreciation for the value of endless conversations and storytelling during teatime. She recognizes that rehashing family history with others is a rich context for cultivating her identity during the psychosocial moratorium.

Erikson (1968) observes that during the moratorium, adolescents often experiment with extreme behaviors, fads, or values before selecting more moderate choices (235–236). Young adult literature illustrates teens' extremism. Several protagonists begin their journey toward identity achievement with a temporary overemphasis upon self-sufficiency. Mary Call, the fourteen-year-old protagonist of Bill and Vera Cleavers' novel *Where the Lilies Bloom* (1969), believes it is better not to ask for help from people outside the family. She organizes the care of her brothers and sisters without relying on others. Mary is trying to fulfill a promise that she made to her father before he died to keep everyone together and never accept charity. She sums up her fierce pride when she thinks to herself, "It's because I'm tough . . . I'm so tough that if a bear came out of the side of the mountain over there I could knock him cold without even breathing hard" (82). Mary and her siblings do not tell others that their father has died. Until circumstances change, they struggle alone to survive life in the mountains. Mary Call and her siblings change during their struggles. Without giving up their independence, they learn about helping one another through connection.

A Balancing Act: Identity Achievement

Expanding upon the work of Erikson and Marcia, psychologists are redefining the core issues of identity achievement. Instead of just emphasizing independence, identity achievement today entails a more complex balance between self-sufficiency and meaningful affiliation with others. Research of Ruthellen Josselson (1994, 83), Carol Gilligan (1988, 3–19), and others indicates that adolescents' independence evolves through close relationships rather than through psychological distance.

By looking inside themselves, talking honestly to others, tackling problems, and developing realistic self-confidence, people in literature and life discover how stronger connections to family and friends provide an integrated sense of self. No longer relying upon physical or emotional distance to establish autonomy, they develop a strong sense of identity and develop closer relationships with others. Thus, identity achievement opens individuals' inner and outer worlds. People who establish a healthy identity have a sense of commitment, yet they are receptive to new experiences. Their openness and conviction stems from a solid sense of self.

I Am Drawn to This Like a Magnet

According to Erik Erikson, people who attain identity gradually discover a cause, goal, or set of values that give purpose and meaning to their lives (Fuhrmann 1990, 359). Erikson (1968) labels this ideological commitment "fidelity" (233, 235). Fidelity is a distinguishing feature of identity achievement. As Erikson describes,

> The evidence in young lives of the search for something and somebody to be true to can be seen in a variety of pursuits more or less sanctioned by society . . . in all youth's seeming shiftiness, a seeking after some durability in change can be detected, whether in the accuracy of scientific and technical method or in the sincerity of obedience; . . . or the fairness in the rules of the game; in the authenticity of artistic production, . . . or in the genuineness of convictions and the reliability of commitments. This search is easily misunderstood, and often it is only dimly perceived by the individual himself. (235)

Fidelity illustrates how individuals can be pulled toward something without fully understanding why until later.

The search for fidelity is illustrated in Elizabeth Speare's *The Witch of Blackbird Pond* (1958). In this novel, a young woman named Kit feels like an alien after she arrives from Barbados to live with her aunt and uncle in a Puritan community of the late 1600s. One day, as she walks with her cousin, she notices the "Great Meadows" for the first time:

> From that first moment, in a way she could never explain, the Meadows claimed her and made her their own. As far as she could see they stretched on either side, a great level sea of green, broken here and there by a solitary graceful elm. Was it the fields of sugar cane they brought to mind, or the endless reach of the ocean to meet the sky? Or was it simply the sense of freedom and space and light that spoke to her of home? (76)

Later, Kit runs to this field when she is upset. Here, she begins to see solutions to her complicated troubles. Eventually, she understands why she is drawn to the Meadows. An older woman named Hannah, who lives there, inspires Kit to find freedom and genuineness even when she is discouraged by the restrictions and reprimands of others in her outer world.

Fidelity surfaces as people develop new philosophies. Virginia Euwer Wolff's *Make Lemonade* (1993) illustrates such a transformation in beliefs. This novel describes the friendship between fourteen-year-old LaVaughn and Jolly, a seventeen-year-old mother of two young children. When Jolly becomes fed up with the hard knocks in her life, she tells LaVaughn a story she has recently heard about an old woman who is blind. The blind woman is attacked one day by a gang of boys who knock her down and steal from her. One boy from the gang offers his hand to help her and hands her back what she believes is her orange. Since she is blind, she does not know immediately that the boy replaced her orange with a lemon. The real kicker is that she thanks this boy. When she discovers the lemon, initially she blames herself for being so naive. However, her anger prompts her to translate adversity into gain. She squeezes juice from the lemon, and adds sugar and water in order to make a drink that will nourish her children. Jolly uses the moral of this story to change her whole approach to adversity.

Someone I Look Up To

Erikson believes that adult guidance is important for fidelity and identity achievement. During middle adolescence, young people may select someone outside the family to emulate because they believe this person has characteristics that they want to develop (Reinecke 1993, 394). They may also worship other individuals outside the family as they de-idealize their parents (Muuss 1988, 62). In literature and life, adult mentors can guide and motivate change in teenagers without dictating, giving sermons, or trivializing concerns. Their conversations with adolescents are influential as they recall family history, describe their own growth, and preserve their cultural heritage. These role models can become symbols of what is possible for a young person.

For example, in Avi's *The True Confessions of Charlotte Doyle* (1990), one man, Zachariah, speaks to the protagonist, Charlotte, of the bravery behind freedom. He says "'A sailor . . . chooses the wind that takes the ship from safe port . . . but winds have a mind of their own'" (226). His words motivate Charlotte to depart from the oppression that she feels in her father's home. Both Charlotte and Zachariah become prisoners while traveling on a long journey by ship. However, they rebel against this slavery and ultimately achieve autonomy.

Adolescents' Self-Understanding

Cultivating independence, maintaining close bonds, developing loyalty, and discovering role models influence self-knowledge. Self-understanding is a complex concept. It includes adolescents' description of themselves in diverse roles. In his recent text, John Santrock (1996) refers to the work of Susan Harter and William Damon, who are well known for their research in this area. In general, studies indicate that adolescents are more likely than children to describe themselves using abstract, idealistic terms. Their self-descriptions also reflect appreciation for their diverse roles in life. Teens understand that they behave differently in numerous contexts (Santrock 1996, 323–325).

During adolescence, young people can recognize that they possess contradictory traits. They are puzzled by these discrepancies but may not resolve them until later (Santrock 1996, 323–324). Adolescents gradually reconcile the disparities between their ideal self (who they would like to be) and their real self (who they really are). The greatest dissimilarity between the ideal and real self occurs during middle adolescence.

These components of teenagers' self-concepts are reflected in Anne Frank's *The Diary of a Young Girl* (1995). She wrote this diary between the ages of thirteen and fifteen. Her own self-description includes abstract qualities:

> I have one outstanding character trait that must be obvious to anyone who's known me for any length of time: I have a great deal of self-knowledge . . . In addition, I face life with an extraordinary amount of courage. I feel so strong and capable of carrying burdens, so young and free! (328–329)

In another excerpt, she describes contradictory aspects of herself when she writes:

> As I've told you many times, I'm split in two. One side contains my exuberant cheerfulness, my flippancy, my joy in life and, above all, my ability to appreciate the lighter side of things. . . . This side of me is usually lying in wait to ambush the other one, which is much purer, deeper and finer. (334–335)

Other entries in her diary highlight the clash between how Anne views herself and how her parents view her.

In Lois Lowry's *A Summer to Die* (1977), the thirteen-year-old protagonist, Meg Chalmers, recognizes that one day she wants to do something worthwhile. She is also aware of the divergence between her real self and ideal self. Meg sees contradictory aspects of herself as well when she thinks "Being both determined and unsure at the same time is what makes me the way I am . . ." (3). This understanding is constructive. It leads to experimentation and self-discovery. Both her family and a friend named Will encourage Meg to develop her talents in photography. Meg obtains additional self-understanding through her important relationships with family and friends.

Young adult novels illustrate how adolescents' self-examination is influenced by their self-esteem. In general, psychologists define self-esteem as individuals' positive or negative view of their own self worth (Santrock 1996, 323, 325). As revealed in *The Diary of a Young Girl*, Anne Frank's positive self-image helps her deal constructively with the conflicts and emotional intensity of adolescence. She recognizes her own strengths and weaknesses and values self-improvement. Anne's self-esteem is nurtured by her family. These resources provide stability and support as she copes with very difficult circumstances.

In contrast, Pecola Breedlove, the female protagonist of Toni Morrison's *The Bluest Eye* (1970), has such a distorted, negative self-image that it is excruciating to witness. This black child yearns for blue eyes to make her beautiful. The brutality in Pecola's life deepens her loss of self-worth. Unlike Anne Frank, Pecola does not have a family that offers emotional support or nurturance. She has little to draw upon for sustenance or hope. Her ultimate destruction is profound. When a person has such a painfully negative self-image, he or she may have little energy or incentive for acquiring self-knowledge. Moreover, when attempts at self-understanding are made, the resulting insights are often distorted because of the level of damage.

Conclusion

Young adult fiction and psychological studies illustrate how identity confusion, identity foreclosure, negative identity and extremism limit our potential in the long term. Like many aspects of psychological strength, identity achievement and self-understanding are not worn like discernible pieces of clothing. People who attain identity and self-knowledge connect their interior world with realistic action in the outside world. However, it is hard to see the thinking and change behind these accomplishments. Examples of the moratorium, fidelity, and self-understanding in literature and psychology underline the value of experimentation and internal probing for identity achievement.

Works Cited

Atwater, E. 1992. *Adolescence.* 3d. ed. Englewood Cliffs, NJ: Prentice-Hall.

Avi. 1990. *The True Confessions of Charlotte Doyle.* New York: Avon Books.

Brooks, B. 1986. *Midnight Hour Encores.* New York: HarperKeypoint.

Cleaver, B., and V. Cleaver. 1969. *Where the Lilies Bloom.* New York: Harper-Keypoint.

Cormier, R. 1979. *After the First Death.* New York: Dell.

————. 1977. *I Am the Cheese.* New York: Dell.

Crutcher, C. 1983. *Running Loose.* New York: Dell.

Dacey, J., and M. Kenny. 1994. *Adolescent Development.* Madison, WI: WCB Brown & Benchmark.

Elkind, D. 1981. *The Hurried Child: Growing Up Too Fast Too Soon.* Reading, MA: Addison-Wesley.

Erikson, E. 1968. *Identity: Youth and Crisis.* New York: W. W. Norton & Company.

Frank, A. 1995. *The Diary of a Young Girl: The Definitive Edition.* Translated by Susan Massotty. Edited by O. H. Frank and M. Pressler. New York: Doubleday.

Fuhrmann, B. S. 1990. *Adolescence, Adolescents.* 2d. ed. Glenview, IL: Scott, Foresman and Company.

Gilligan, C. 1988. "Remapping the Moral Domain: New Images of Self in Relationship." In *Mapping the Moral Domain: A Contribution of Women's Thinking to Psychological Theory and Education,* eds., C. Gilligan, J. V. Ward, J. M. Taylor, with B. Bardige, 3–19. Cambridge, MA: Harvard University Press.

Hinton, S. E. 1967. *The Outsiders.* New York: Dell.

Josselson, R. 1994. "Identity and Relatedness in the Life Cycle." In *Identity and Development: An Interdisciplinary Approach,* edited by H. A. Bosma, T. G. Graafsma, H. Grotevant, and D. J. de Levita, 81–102. Thousand Oaks, CA: Sage.

Lowry, L. 1977. *A Summer to Die.* New York: Dell.

Marcia, J. 1980. "Identity in Adolescence." In *Handbook of Adolescent Psychology,* edited by J. Adelson, 159–187. New York: John Wiley.

————. 1994. "The Empirical Study of Ego Identity." In *Identity and Development: An Interdisciplinary Approach,* edited by H. A. Bosma, T. L. G. Graafsma, H. D. Grotevant, and D. J. de Levita, 67–80. Thousand Oaks, CA: Sage.

Morrison, T. 1970. *The Bluest Eye.* New York: Plume.

Muuss, R. E. 1988. *Theories of Adolescence.* 5th ed. New York: Random House.

Pipher, M. 1994. *Reviving Ophelia: Saving the Selves of Adolescent Girls.* New York: Ballantine Books.

Reinecke, M. A. 1993. "Outpatient Treatment of Mild Psychopathology." In *Handbook of Clinical Research and Practice with Adolescents*, edited by P. H. Tolan and B. J. Cohler, 387–410. New York: John Wiley & Sons.

Rice, F. P. 1996. *The Adolescent: Development, Relationships and Culture*. 8th ed. Boston: Allyn & Bacon.

Ruckman, I. 1988. *No Way Out*. New York: HarperKeypoint.

Santrock, J. W. 1996. *Adolescence: An Introduction*. 6th ed. Madison, WI: Brown & Benchmark Publishers.

Speare, E. G. 1958. *The Witch of Blackbird Pond*. New York: Dell.

Steinberg, L. 1983. *Adolescence*. 3d ed. New York: McGraw-Hill.

Thesman, J. 1991. *The Rain Catchers*. New York: Avon Books.

Voigt, C. 1981. *Homecoming*. New York: Ballantine Books.

———. 1982. *Dicey's Song*. New York: Bantam Books.

Wolff, V. E. 1993. *Make Lemonade*. New York: Scholastic.

Zindel, P. 1968. *The Pigman*. Toronto: Bantam.

Two

Home, Where I Grow Up

The best way out is always through.

Perhaps each one of us feels like an orphan at some point in our lives. Something is missing at home. Or, we feel we cannot go home again after a journey because we are not the same person. People fend for themselves, survive a difficult loss in their family, or search for answers to mysteries about the past. As orphans, our journey includes finding a new home and negotiating a complex balance between separation and connection. Initially, we can establish independence through our behaviors or through physical separation from family. Yet, many of us discover more intricate, psychological sides of autonomy. Achieving independence occurs by changing important relationships with others.

What Psychologists Say About Family Relationships

For many years, research emphasized that family relationships were very stressful during the adolescence of a family member. Traditional models also highlighted teenagers' rebellion against parental influence. Psychoanalytic views, in particular, underlined that conflict was necessary for adolescents to gain autonomy (Cobb 1995, 210–212). Lack of conflict signaled delays in teenagers' separation and independence.

Today, a different perspective on family relationships exists in contemporary psychological research. Although there is increased conflict and stress during early adolescence, the majority of parents and adolescents report positive relationships (Steinberg 1993, 131, 139). Disputes increase during the peak changes of puberty, and mothers as well as fathers often experience considerable stress when their oldest child reaches puberty (Steinberg and Steinberg 1994, 15–63). Parent-adolescent disagreements center upon everyday matters such as chores, curfews, and social activities. The discord serves a useful purpose, enabling teenagers to establish their autonomy within close family relationships.

I'm in a Tug-of-War

A recurring theme in young adult literature and adolescent psychological studies is that intimacy and autonomy evolve as positive outcomes of conflict and connection in parent-child relations. Cultures also vary in their definitions of autonomy; some emphasize individuals' independence more than family cohesion. Adolescents feel the tension between these emphases as they separate from parents. Establishing autonomy has dramatic impact on the quality of relationships outside the family.

As Cooper and Grotevant (cited in Steinberg 1993, 146) and other investigators (Gilligan 1982, 5–23) explain, separation and connection are closely intertwined with adolescents' attainment of autonomy, identity development, and moral development. Cooper and Grotevant's research indicates that autonomous individuals willingly voice their own opinion, even if it differs from other family members' views. They also respect other people's ideas, feel separate, and yet are emotionally attached to others.

A number of psychoanalytic thinkers, including Ruthellen Josselson (1980, 190–197), label this tension between separation and connection as "individuation." As Josselson describes, individuation is a complex process. Generally, it refers to adolescents' separation from family and the development of a clear sense of individuality. During the subphases of individuation, adolescents may repudiate parents' guidance as well as find ingenious ways to vex or oppose their mothers and fathers. Teens' tendency towards omnipotency combined with their sense of invulnerability/immortality can lead them to overlook precautions. Gradually, adolescents redefine cooperative relationships with their parents based on a new sense of self as a distinct, separate person (Seifert and Hoffnung 1994, 546–548). Individuation is a lifelong process (Josselson 1980, 191) and will even influence peer relations.

The Ordinary Matters: Separation

People achieve individuation gradually through daily decisions (Cobb 1995, 226). Achieving this process through close relationships rather than through distancing, adolescents gain new freedom; however, they may also experience fear or ambivalence (Josselson 1980, 195; Seifert and Hoffnung 1994, 548; Steinberg 1993, 293). Separation occurs through the adolescents' disagreements, daily hassles with parents, experimentation, risk taking, and increased involvement with peers.

In Suzanne Newton's *I Will Call It Georgie's Blues* (1983), the protagonist, Neal, describes how he avoided family conflict at an earlier time:

> When I was younger I read in a magazine: "In order to make mealtimes pleasant one should discuss topics that are conflict-free." I spent days trying to think up topics that were conflict-free, but finally gave up. Everything—even sunflowers and white mice—leads to tears and shouting, or else silence, which is worse. I have concluded that the conflict is there, like it or not, and it will ride on any words that are spoken. So my contribution to family tranquility is to keep my mouth shut. (14)

Later, Neal defies his father's expectation that he would mow the churchyard without pay and recalls how it felt to speak up for what he wanted. "Some little boy part of me fully expected to hear his footsteps thundering up the stairs in pursuit, but nothing happened. My heart was pounding so hard I had trouble breathing" (53).

In *The Diary of a Young Girl* (1995), Anne Frank describes the conflict she has with her mother:

> I was furious at mother (and still am a lot of the time). It's true, she didn't understand me, but I didn't understand her either. Because she loved me, she was tender and affectionate, but because of the difficult situations I put her in, and the sad circumstances in which she found herself, she was nervous and irritable, so I can understand why she was often short with me. (158–59)

At this time, Anne has the maturity to take her mother's perspective as she sorts through her complex feelings about their disagreements.

The Balance: Connection on New Terms

In her text *Adolescence*, author Nancy Cobb (1995) describes how family members establish connection by developing joint respect and receptivity to the views of others (citing Cooper and Grotevant, 229–233). Overall, research indicates that relationships between parents and teenagers become more cooperative and closer after puberty and during late adolescence. Excessive rebellion and prolonged detachment from the family delay autonomy and individuation (Kroger 1989, 57; Steinberg 1993, 139, 293).

There are vivid examples in young adult literature of adolescents' struggle to balance separation and connection in family relationships. In Cynthia Voigt's novels *Homecoming* (1981) and *Dicey's Song* (1982), the Tillerman children are on their own as they travel in search of a home. Dicey supervises her siblings during their long journey. After they find a home with their grandmother, Dicey is initially reserved and distant from new classmates who want to become her friend. Dicey's grandmother recognizes herself in this stubborn, independent granddaughter who doesn't get too close to anyone. She guides Dicey to avoid the pitfalls of overlearned independence when she says "... you have to reach out to people. To your family too. You can't just let them sit there, you should put your hand out. If they slap it back, well you reach out again if you care enough" (Voigt 1982, 128).

How difficult it is to negotiate this delicate balance between separation and connection! The lifelong struggle is reflected in Dicey's question to her grandmother, "You tell me to let go. But you told me to reach out, you told me to hold on. How can I do all those things together? Gram?" (Voigt 1982, 202). This grandmother does not want Dicey to repeat her own lonely path of pushing away her family and friends because she is hurt and angry.

Sue Ellen Bridgers' *Permanent Connections* (1981) also illustrates the process of separation and connection. In the beginning of this novel, the protagonist, Rob, is angry and rebellious. His encounters with the police after an accident, his experimentation with drugs, his antagonistic relationships with family and relatives alienate him from others. Eventually, Rob's reckless behavior and careless attitude toward people leads to a serious accident. The incident forces him to recognize how much he has hurt himself and family members. He begins a painful process of accepting full responsibility for his actions, addressing his problems, and accepting help from others. At the end of the novel, he appreciates the love and care of his family, relatives, and friends, and no longer pushes them away. For the first time in his life, Rob has a sense of direction.

I Am an Orphan

Young adult fiction includes many stories of families in which one or both parents are missing from home (Greenway 1991, 15–17; Nadeau 1995, 14–17). In Bruce Brooks' *Midnight Hour Encores* (1986), and Jean Thesman's *The Rain Catchers* (1991), mothers leave their families because they did not think they could manage childrearing or felt overwhelmed. In other stories, such as *Homecoming, Dicey's Song,* Sue Ellen Bridgers' *Notes for Another Life* (1981), and Vera and Bill Cleaver's *Where the Lilies Bloom* (1989), parents are unavailable because of emotional illness or death. Additional stories with absent parents in young adult literature include Robert Cormier's *I Am the Cheese* (1977), Katherine Paterson's *The Great Gilly Hopkins* (1978), and Alice Childress' *Rainbow Jordan* (1981).

Parents' physical or psychological departure can force young people to begin a search, to change, and to become more responsible. Orphans such as Adam Farmer of *I Am the Cheese* feel as if they have no identity because they lack information about the past. In *Midnight Hour Encores* and *The Rain Catchers,* daughters search for their mothers. They want to develop their own identity by further exploring their family backgrounds. Other orphans become parents to younger siblings in order to survive. After they find safety and trust, they abdicate that role and reach out to other people.

Why are there so many absent family members in young adult fiction? First, missing parents and children in young adult literature may reflect the fragmentation of family in our society today through violence, death, illness, and divorce. Disorder inside and outside the home, as well as pressure on families, make it harder for adolescents to attain independence in the context of close relationships. Second, the orphans of young adult fiction reveal how young people can be pushed to grow up too quickly in our culture. Psychologists trace a parallel phenomenon in child and adolescent psychology. Third, parental absence in young adult novels may mirror mothers' or fathers' emotional unavailability to their children in some families. This detachment resembles psychologists' description of the permissive-indifferent or neglectful style of parenting. Although they are physically present, these parents remain distant, cold, and unresponsive in their daily interactions with their children (Maccoby and Martin 1983, 48–49).

Fourth, the prevalence of orphans in young adult literature lends validity to David Elkind's (1981) description of teenagers' belief in the personal fable (114–115). Most often, this component of egocentrism is defined as adolescents' exaggerated view of their own uniqueness. It is a common theme in young people's conversations and journals, reflected in statements such as "Nobody could possibly understand." Psychologists link adolescents' risk taking to the personal fable. The personal fable also includes young adults' tendency to fabricate a story about their own upbringing or history. Therefore, teens may wonder temporarily whether they are adopted or whether they are an orphan (Sprinthall and Collins 1995, 153). Newton's *I Will Call It Georgie's Blues* (1983) illustrates such a belief. In this story, the protagonist Neal talks to his younger brother Georgie, who feels that his ". . . Mom and Dad are false" (87). Until Neal understands Georgie's thinking more fully, he initially wonders if Georgie believes he is adopted. He reassures Georgie that he once believed the same thing and tells him it is normal to feel this way at his age.

Similarly, in *The Diary of A Young Girl* (1995), Anne Frank writes about her own temporary fantasy of being an orphan:

> Before I came here, when I didn't think about things as much as I do now, I occasionally had the feeling that I didn't belong to Momsy, Pim and Margot and that I would always be an outsider. I sometimes went around for six months at a time pretending I was an orphan. Then I'd chastise myself for playing the victim, when really, I'd always been so fortunate. (168)

A fifth explanation is that the striking frequency of orphans and missing parents in young adult literature may also represent the various phases of individuation. Most often, in these novels, adolescents establish a temporary psychological distance or permanent physical distance from family. This separation enables them to gain unusual experiences. During their journey, they develop a new vision of themselves and the world. When they do return home, their relationships are based on new terms.

The "Orphan's" Journey Begins with Rare Vision

What I label "rare vision" for the protagonists of young adult fiction is what makes each person's reality (his or her inner and outer world) unique and different from other people's reality. It includes adolescents' exposure to unique events within the family or in other situations that trigger intense feelings. The vision makes them feel set apart from others. Overall, it is a source of liberation but can raise disturbing insights as well. Thus, some "orphans" mature as a result of their rare vision. Others flee when they gain new information.

Many young adult novels illustrate how "orphans" or protagonists who face significant life crises can develop unique vision. An adolescent female is a victim of terrorism in Robert Cormier's *After the First Death* (1979). Another young woman has a car accident in Cynthia Voigt's *Izzy, Willy-Nilly* (1986). Teenagers lose a loved one through death in Chris Crutcher's *Running Loose* (1983) and Will Hobbs' *Changes in Latitudes* (1988). Alternatively, a person may gain inside knowledge or disclose something for the first time. This change occurs in Robert Cormier's *Fade*, Lois Lowry's *The Giver* (1993), Chris Crutcher's *Chinese Handcuffs* (1983), and Jacqueline Woodson's *I Hadn't Meant to Tell You This* (1994).

Young adult fiction often portrays how rare vision can be terrifying as well as emancipating. In *Fade*, Paul discovers his unusual ability to become invisible. Mesmerized by this skill, he uncovers disturbing family secrets and witnesses other harrowing scenes. His exposure to the underbelly of society changes him forever. In *The Giver*, the protagonist, Jonas, also develops rare vision. During a special apprenticeship with his teacher, the Giver, he begins to experience intense emotions and recalls lost memories for a colorless society. Eventually, Jonas is so troubled by the chilling activities of this regimented community that he plots an escape. Both Paul and Jonas feel like oddballs and contemplate whether their unique perspective is a curse or gift.

Unusual vision can be a source of fear and renewal, as illustrated in Zibby Oneal's *The Language of Goldfish* (1980). Carrie, the protagonist, has a vivid and unusual glimpse of a fantasy world from childhood. It stems from a conversation with her sister when they talk about the goldfish in their backyard pond. They pretend the goldfish can bring them to the safe retreat of a little island at the center of their pond. Carrie's vision is linked to her withdrawal from the demands of adolescence and adulthood. Her feelings of alienation and isolation become so strong that she attempts suicide. Yet, as Carrie recovers, this vision changes and eventually stimulates her art. Carrie's perspective is finally expressed in a beautiful painting of the island.

Overall, "orphans'" rare vision can be linked to psychologists' description of adolescents' belief in their own uniqueness (the personal fable) and to the process of separation-individuation. It also accompanies the de-idealization of parents. As David Elkind (1981, 107) and others (Steinberg 1993, 292) explain, when adolescents separate from their families, they no longer see their parents as infallible. Their subsequent search can involve detecting how they will differ from their parents or escape conformity. Eventually, young people also incorporate their new perspective with more realistic views of themselves and their families.

Family Resemblances: Mirror on the Wall

As a result of individuation, adolescents and parents view each other in a different light. There are times in our life when we are struck by family resemblances. Yet, initially, young adolescents can exaggerate how different they are from their parents by adopting unusual points of view, styles of dress, haircuts, language codes, music, body pins, or other accessories (Steinberg and Levine 1990, 185). In *The Diary of a Young Girl* (1995), Anne Frank writes about how different she is from her parents:

I'm the opposite of Mother, so of course we clash. I don't mean to judge her; I don't have that right. I'm simply looking at her as a mother. She's not a mother to me—I have to mother myself. I've cut myself adrift from them. I'm charting my own course. . . . (63)

In Bridgers' *Notes for Another Life* (1981), one of the protagonists, Wren, emphasizes at one point that she will be different from her own mother, Karen. This young woman believes "She wouldn't be like Karen, giving up husband and children for a career. She wouldn't abandon infants, expecting them to love her anyway, in spite of all the emptiness she left" (157). Later, Wren notices more complexities in decisions about family and career. When she recognizes her own ambitions, she considers the hard choices her mother made. When adolescents become more independent, they increasingly value their parents as individual people.

As parents watch their sons and daughters gain autonomy, their vision changes too. Parents see aspects of themselves in their own children and also perceive the differences. For example, in Bridgers' *Permanent Connections* (1987), Ginny sees the changes in her daughter Ellery and reflects on what it is like to raise children: ". . . her mind took her elsewhere, back into her own childhood, then forward into Ellery's. Sometimes lately she confused the two, couldn't distinguish the child from the mother, as if she were living her young life again in Ellery. How could that be when they were so different?" (71–72). Ginny draws a parallel between her weaving on her loom and her parenting:

Her foot pushed the treadle, the harness went up, the shuttle made its journey, the beater brought the reed forward again. The loom groaned as it moved, gathering the pattern she had set while she and her daughter wove the hurts into a song devoid of harmony but played together just the same. (74)

In Lois Lowry's *A Summer to Die* (1977), one daughter, Meg, notices how her mother sees herself in Meg's sister, Molly. Meg observes:

When Mom looks at Molly, her memories go back farther, to her own self as a girl, because they are so alike, and it must be a puzzling thing to see yourself growing up again. It must be like looking through the wrong end of a telescope—seeing yourself young, far away, on your own; the distance is too great for the watcher, really, to do anything more than watch, and remember, and smile. (14–15)

The change in vision for adolescents as well as parents influences discipline in the home. For example, in Judith Guest's *Ordinary People* (1970), a father and son renegotiate their relationship. The son, Conrad Jarrett, is living at home with his parents after being hospitalized for a suicide attempt. Conrad sees a psychiatrist and gradually resolves his intense feelings regarding his brother's death. As Conrad becomes healthier, his relationship with his father improves. Eventually, his dad sees the psychiatrist for help with his own problems. This father and son become more open and expressive. In the past, Conrad's father was fearful of saying something that would upset his son. When Conrad's father directly expresses his anger about a comment Conrad makes, Conrad apologizes and says "You were right. You ought to do that [express anger and set limits] more often" (238). It is clear that both father and son view each other on new, healthier terms.

The Different Sides of My Autonomy

Within this context, adolescents achieve different types of autonomy (Atwater 1992, 139–140; Steinberg 1993, 289–292). Behavioral autonomy requires the ability to implement and follow through on decisions. It also includes competent performance of age-appropriate behaviors and accomplishments. Working effectively at a job, handling increased responsibility at home, and gaining financial independence illustrate aspects of behavioral autonomy for adolescents.

As psychologists explain, emotional autonomy develops more slowly than behavioral autonomy. It is valuable and involves transforming key relationships, especially with parents, rather than ending or minimizing ties. Overall, it requires the person's ability to use his or her own inner resiliency when facing setbacks, hurdles, or defeat (Atwater 1992, 140). Individuals who handle feedback, frustrations, or difficult challenges constructively have developed emotional autonomy.

Laurence Steinberg and colleagues describe four different components of emotional autonomy (Steinberg 1993, 291–292). One aspect is the de-idealization of parents. This "dethroning" partially explains why adolescents become more critical of their parents during early adolescence. A second component of emotional autonomy involves increased self-reliance; teenagers become more adept at addressing their own problems and handling responsibilities. A third component centers upon young people's sense of individuation and separateness from their parents. For example, they can disagree with their parents and acknowledge that their parents do not know everything about them and vice versa. The fourth component enables adolescents to appreciate their parents as individuals beyond their role as caregivers. This dimension may not be fully acquired until young adulthood.

There are examples in young adult fiction of adolescents who gradually attain emotional autonomy. In Terry Davis' *If Rock and Roll Were a Machine* (1992), the protagonist, Bert Bowden, develops increased emotional autonomy. Initially, he becomes angry and gives up easily when learning racquetball. With an adult mentor's guidance, he gradually sets realistic goals, handles the frustrations of the game, and eventually faces a former adversary in competition.

How easy it is to overlook the emotional autonomy of individuals. In Elizabeth Speare's *The Witch of Blackbird Pond* (1958), the protagonist, Kit, notices how much inner strength her cousin Mercy has. Others view Mercy as weak because she is lame. Kit sees Mercy differently:

> Mercy certainly did not consider herself afflicted. She did a full day's work and more. Moreover, Kit had soon discovered that Mercy was the pivot about whom the whole household moved. She coaxed her father out of his bitter moods, upheld her timorous and anxious mother, gently restrained her rebellious sister and had reached to draw an uncertain alien into the circle. Mercy weak! (64)

Other protagonists of young adult literature develop increased emotional autonomy. This change is illustrated in Paterson's *The Great Gilly Hopkins* (1978). As a foster child, Gilly never allows herself to become attached to other people. Moving from one home to another, she deliberately antagonizes people at home and school. Always plotting to escape, Gilly fires off an angry letter to her mother, who lives in California. The letter falsely portrays the conditions in Gilly's new foster home as dismal. Then, without any preplanning, Gilly becomes very attached to her foster mother, Trotter, and the little boy who lives with Trotter. However, her letter eventually leads to consequences that force Gilly to leave Trotter's home. This warm, caring foster mother reminds Gilly that the key to her own happiness lies in how well Gilly can respond to difficult circumstances.

In Oneal's *The Language of Goldfish* (1980), Carrie's relationship with her parents changes as she becomes healthier and attains emotional independence. Carrie is gifted and yet she has much difficulty accepting the changes of adolescence. This novel describes Carrie's gradual recovery from her suicide attempt as she develops more meaningful relationships with family and peers at home and school through the help of a psychiatrist, her art teacher, family, and friends. She recognizes her mother's use of denial while discussing psychological illness. Yet, over time, Carrie's relationship with her mother changes. She no longer withdraws or runs away from conflicts or problems at school.

Disciplinary Action

Psychological studies and young adult literature illustrate that adolescence is a critical stage of development for parents and their teenagers. Youths as well as parents face key issues related to identity achievement, physical development, and social growth. Both generations are agents of change.

In research on families, psychologists frequently cite the work of Diana Baumrind, a pioneer in studying different styles of parenting, which she labeled *authoritative, authoritarian,* and *permissive.* She defines these parenting styles based on two key dimensions. One dimension is the degree of responsivity or acceptance that parents display. The second is the amount of the parents' control over or demands made on their children or adolescents. Parents often rely on a blend of disciplinary techniques (Santrock 1996, 184–186). The overall atmosphere in the home and parents' general pattern of discipline have a key impact on families' long-term adjustment (Maccoby and Martin 1983, 39–50; Steinberg 1993, 141–145).

Researchers link the authoritative style of discipline to the most positive outcomes. Authoritative parents are warm and responsive with their sons and daughters, yet they also use firm guidance. This style of parenting includes flexibility and has favorable effects on adolescents' social competence and academic achievement. Young adult literature portrays the realistic fluctuation in parents' effective childrearing styles as they cope with important changes in their sons and daughters. This genre also illustrates the reciprocal influence of adolescents on their parents.

For example, Gary Paulsen's *Sentries* (1986) describes the coming of age of one adolescent girl named Laura, who catalyzes changes in her own parents' restrictions. Laura has loved lambing since childhood. For the first time, Laura's parents want her to quit lambing in order to attend school. As Paulsen tells us:

> Her father was what Laura thought of as a one-way kind of person, hard outside sometimes but usually fair. Almost always fair. But when he said a thing, that's the way it was and the way it stayed and Laura would have to be cautious about changing anything. And she meant to make a change. She was being cut out of things or felt she was, and she meant to change that. (42)

Later, she and her father talk, and she is able to voice how she feels about wanting to lamb. Her father recognizes and validates Laura's opinions and rights: ". . . your mama and me, we talked it over and she said I was wrong. That you are part of this, part of all that I started as much as I am, and it would be wrong to push you away even if I thought it was right, even if I thought it was for your own good" (154–155). Laura feels fortunate to have a father like him.

In Lois Duncan's *Daughters of Eve* (1979), the conversations of one of the protagonists, Ann, with her father are based on warmth and respect. When Ann faces a difficult decision, her father uses an authoritative approach to guide her: "Annie, . . . this is your own life you're leading. Nobody else can live it for you. You've got to decide things the way you think they'll be best" (243).

In contrast, strict, harsh discipline and authoritarian parenting are associated with less optimal outcomes for adolescents. Teenagers' awareness of the differences between authoritative and authoritarian styles of parenting is illustrated in Crutcher's *Running Loose* (1983). Louie Banks, the protagonist, describes the complementary influence of his father, Norm, and his mother, Brenda. He notes:

> Anyway, except for the times I wish I had crappy parents so I'd have someone to blame things on, I gotta say I got a pretty good deal. Norm's always real calm and takes time to work things out. Doesn't like to leave a lot of loose ends. He's a good guy to go to when you have a problem. He'll never tell you the answer, but he'll stick with you till you come up with one. Brenda's a little more emotional— like to the seventh power—but you need a little of that . . .
>
> Don't get me wrong. We don't live here like the Beaver Cleaver family or the Waltons all the time. Brenda and I go at it pretty regularly. (25–26)

Louie knows another boy, Boomer, whose father would "whip the crap out of him" (13). He can see the effect it has on Boomer, who physically threatens others.

Additional studies document the effects of two different types of permissive parenting (Maccoby and Martin 1983, 39–50). One type is labeled *permissive-indulgent* and the other is labeled *permissive-indifferent*. Permissive-indulgent parents are overly tolerant of their children's misbehavior. They are warm but do not make any demands of their children. In contrast, permissive-indifferent parents are rejecting and unresponsive with their children.

Susan Hinton's *The Outsiders* (1967) illustrates how young people who join gangs have often been raised in hostile or permissive homes. Several boys who belong to a gang named the Greasers have taken special care of a boy named Johnny, whose parents are openly antagonistic toward him. They recognize how much it has hurt Johnny and that no matter how much they try, the gang just cannot substitute completely for family. Another boy, Randy, who belongs to the Greaser's rival gang, laments the type of home that led one of his friends to adopt a life on the streets:

> They spoiled him rotten. I mean most parents would be proud of a kid like that—good-lookin' and smart and everything, but they gave in to him all the time. He kept trying to make someone say "No" and they never did. They never did. That was what he wanted. For somebody to tell him "No." To have somebody lay down the law, set the limits, give him something solid to stand on. That's what we all want, really. (102)

In my classes, I have heard parents, teachers, and students describe similar, harmful effects of parental detachment.

Conclusion

Literature and psychology underline the hard work behind self-reliance. Both disciplines reveal how detachment constricts our inner and outer world. It is vital to successfully negotiate the complex process of separation and autonomy. The lifelong themes that often originate in our families not only can set us apart from others but also can provide important connections to people.

Works Cited

Atwater, E. 1992. *Adolescence*. 3d ed. Englewood Cliffs, NJ: Prentice-Hall.

Bridgers, S. E. 1981. *Notes for Another Life*. New York: Bantam Books.

———. 1987. *Permanent Connections*. New York: HarperKeypoint.

Brooks, B. 1986. *Midnight Hour Encores*. New York: HarperKeypoint.

Childress, A. 1981. *Rainbow Jordan*. New York: Avon.

Cleaver, V., and B. Cleaver. 1969. *Where the Lilies Bloom*. New York: Harper-Keypoint.

Cobb, N. J. 1995. *Adolescence: Continuity, Change, and Diversity*. 2d ed. Mountain View, CA: Mayfield.

Cormier, R. 1977. *I Am the Cheese*. New York: Dell.

———. 1979. *After the First Death*. New York: Dell.

———. 1988. *Fade*. New York: Dell.

Crutcher, C. 1983. *Running Loose*. New York: Dell.

———. 1989. *Chinese Handcuffs*. New York: Dell.

Davis, T. 1992. *If Rock and Roll Were a Machine*. New York: Dell.

Duncan, L. 1979. *Daughters of Eve*. New York: Dell.

Elkind, D. 1981. *The Hurried Child: Growing Up Too Fast, Too Soon*. Reading, MA: Addison-Wesley.

Frank, A. 1995. *The Diary of a Young Girl: The Definitive Edition*. Translated by Susan Massotty. Edited by O. H. Frank and M. Pressler. New York: Doubleday.

Gilligan, C. 1982. *In a Different Voice: Psychological Theory and Women's Development*. Cambridge, MA: Harvard University Press.

Greenway, B. 1991. "Every Mother's Dream: Cynthia Voigt's Orphans." *The Alan Review* 19(1)(Fall): 15–17.

Guest, J. 1976. *Ordinary People*. New York: Ballantine Books.

Hinton, S. 1967. *The Outsiders*. New York: Dell.

Hobbs, W. 1988. *Changes in Latitudes*. New York: Avon Books.

Josselson, R. 1980. "Ego Development in Adolescence." In *Handbook of Adolescent Psychology*, edited by J. Adelson, 188–210. New York: John Wiley & Sons.

Kroger, J. 1989. *Identity in Adolescence: The Balance Between Self and Other*. London: Routledge.

Lowry, L. 1977. *A Summer to Die*. New York: Dell.

———. 1993. *The Giver*. New York: Bantam Doubleday Dell Books.

Maccoby, E. E., and J. A. Martin. 1983. "Socialization in the Context of the Family: Parent-Child Interaction." In *Socialization, Personality, and Social Development*, edited by E. Mavis Hetherington, Handbook of Child Psychology, Vol. 4, 1–101. New York: Wiley.

Nadeau, F. A. 1995. "The Mother-Daughter Relationship in Young Adult Fiction." *The Alan Review* 22(2)(Winter): 14–17.

Newton, S. 1983. *I Will Call It Georgie's Blues*. New York: Penguin Books.

Oneal, Z. 1980. *The Language of Goldfish*. New York: Puffin Books.

Paterson, K. 1978. *The Great Gilly Hopkins*. New York: HarperTrophy.

Paulsen, G. 1986. *Sentries*. New York: Penguin Books.

Santrock, J. 1996. *Adolescence: An Introduction*. 6th ed. Madison, WI: Brown & Benchmark.

Seifert, K. L., and R. J. Hoffnung. 1994. *Child and Adolescent Development*. 3d ed. Boston: Houghton Mifflin.

Speare, E. 1958. *The Witch of Blackbird Pond*. New York: Dell.

Sprinthall, N. A., and W. A. Collins. 1995. *Adolescent Psychology: A Developmental View*. 3d ed. New York: McGraw-Hill.

Steinberg, L. 1993. *Adolescence*. 3d ed. New York: McGraw-Hill.

Steinberg, L., and A. Levine, A. 1990. *You and Your Adolescent: A Parent's Guide for Ages Ten to Twenty*. New York: Harper & Row.

Steinberg, L., and W. Steinberg. 1994. *Crossing Paths: How Your Child's Adolescence Triggers Your Own Crisis*. New York: Simon & Schuster.

Thesman, J. 1991. *The Rain Catchers*. New York: Avon.

Voigt, C. 1981. *Homecoming*. New York: Ballantine Books.

———. 1982. *Dicey's Song*. New York: Ballantine Books.

———. 1986. *Izzy, Willy-Nilly*. New York: Aladdin Paperbacks.

Woodson, J. 1994. *I Hadn't Meant to Tell You This*. New York: Bantam Doubleday Dell Books.

Three

Friends Through Thick and Thin

Still—in a way—nobody sees a flower—really—it is so small—we haven't time—and to see takes time, like to have a friend takes time.

Georgia O'Keeffe

Young adult literature and current research in adolescent psychology present a balanced picture of the positive and negative influence of peer groups on teenagers' development. Examining this literature and research allows us to identify cultural myths about peer influence and recognize the positive effects of adolescent friendships. It also allows us to examine adolescent conformity and to explore the impact of intimidation on young teens.

Discussing these topics in young adult literature offers teachers and students opportunities to explore the temporary effects, long-term benefits, and costs of popularity, friendships, and conformity. Until we have knowledge of and experience with good relationships, we may not always detect the signs of unhealthy, harmful affiliations. Discussing peer influence in different disciplines can help people of any age to develop more realistic concepts of healthy interpersonal relationships and to learn effective ways to resist peer pressure.

What Psychologists Say About Peer Relationships

Developing social competence with peers is valuable for the continual, healthy adjustment of children, adolescents, and adults. A history of peer rejection and problems of aggression can signal long-term difficulties (Sprinthall and Collins 1995, 294). Peers have tremendous influence on teenagers. As adolescents separate from their families, they have increased contact with friends and acquaintances who offer opportunities for developing reciprocal relationships, enhancing moral development, sharpening cognitive skills, and attaining an identity.

There are common myths about peer associations during adolescence. One misconception is that peers always create harmful consequences for teenagers. Current studies indicate that although peers can be a negative influence for adolescents, they can also have a positive impact as well. These effects are bidirectional. Adolescents actually perceive more peer pressure against misbehavior or socially unacceptable acts (Berndt and Savin-Williams 1993, 206). Young adult literature accurately portrays peers' reciprocal influence. The novels also provide vivid examples of the positive impact of friends and illustrate why conformity or intimidation occur.

Another stereotype is that peer groups overshadow parents' guidance during adolescence. Research indicates that friends do not usurp parents' impact on teenagers. Instead, mothers, fathers, and peers have complementary influences on young adults. Parents have a stronger influence on adolescents' decisions regarding education, career, and morality. Peers have relatively stronger impact on adolescents' choices regarding current social issues such as music, dress, and other activities (Cobb 1995, 284; Steinberg and Levine 1990, 181). Young adult fiction realistically depicts parent and peer relationships with teenagers.

Popularity: Today Is Forever

Young adolescents seek peer approval as they separate from their families and respond to society's emphases on social comparison and prestige. These responses offer important opportunities for growth and change. During adolescence, popularity among peers can produce feelings of elation and well-being. Lack of popularity can lead to intense loneliness, rejection, and alienation. The importance of popularity during early adolescence is accentuated by teenagers' belief that "now is forever." They often perceive that their current circumstances and feelings are permanent. This common perception parallels Mary Pipher's description of adolescents' black-and-white thinking (1994, 59).

Increased maturity enables people to appreciate that many situations and experiences are temporary. Popularity in a peer group can shift depending on the leadership, current fads, and other circumstances. There is a cost to prolonged, excessive conformity. Feeling like the outcast or being shunned by cliques during adolescence would be far more tolerable if teenagers understood how group norms and social status can change.

Our Inner and Outer World Mirror Each Other

What Psychologists Say About Adolescents' Friendships

Psychological studies describe how we often attract friends who are similar to us in values, attitudes, and demographic characteristics (Berndt and Savin-Williams 1993, 205). Our friends also reflect our inner world. Through the comfort and solace that surface in close relationships, adolescents as well as adults can derive rich learning experiences from their friends.

Friendships change from childhood to adolescence. Harry Stack Sullivan and others propose that developing closeness in same sex friends ("chums") during childhood and adolescence is instrumental for developing intimacy in subsequent relationships (Kimmel and Weiner 1995, 41, 282; Santrock 1996, 226; Sprinthall and Collins 1995, 303). Preschool children focus on sharing possessions and activities in their friendships, whereas children of middle childhood emphasize trust (Berk 1993, 362, 473). Gossip is important to preadolescents (Cobb, 259–261). In contrast, adolescent friendships center upon self-disclosure and loyalty (Cobb 1995, 263). Teens in middle adolescence place a strong emphasis on keeping confidences, being loyal, and being trustworthy—qualities that add a poignant intensity to friendships. However, this intensity also produces more unstable affiliations. During late adolescence, relationships become less passionate and more stable as individuals develop emotional autonomy (Atwater 1992, 157). These changes enable adolescents as well as adults to cultivate more intimacy with partners.

Inside Our Hearts: We Are More Alike Than We Realized

Friends may be drawn to each other because of a similarity in their backgrounds. Jacqueline Woodson's *I Hadn't Meant to Tell You This* (1994) is a moving portrayal of the close companionship between two girls, Marie and Lena. Marie, who is black, defies her clique's rules by developing a new relationship with Lena, whom adults as well as peers label "white trash." One of the similarities between the girls is that neither has a mother living at home. Lena and Marie talk about this link. By building trust and loyalty, the friendship enables both girls to develop inner strength and come to terms with their mothers' absence.

Helping Each Other to Change

Young adult literature also demonstrates the beauty and power of friendships to help people change and grow in positive ways without deliberate crusades. In Virginia Wolff's *Make Lemonade* (1993), LaVaughn and Jolly develop a close friendship. LaVaughn is reliable, dedicated to her studies, and organized. Jolly, a teenage mother of two small children, struggles to survive with low-paying jobs and few resources. Her life is chaotic. LaVaughn responds to Jolly's advertisement for a job in child care and begins to baby-sit for Jolly's children. Although neither deliberately tries to change the other, LaVaughn and Jolly both mature and grow through their friendship. They fight when LaVaughn becomes exasperated and criticizes Jolly. The conflict tests their friendship but brings them closer. LaVaughn increasingly appreciates the children's perspective and values Jolly's strengths. She also gains valuable knowledge about life and becomes less judgmental. Jolly gains self-confidence, returns to school, and becomes determined to improve her life.

I Like You Just the Way You Are

Friends can also help people appreciate their own unique qualities and see the merits of sensitivity. In Susan Hinton's *The Outsiders* (1967), Johnny and Ponyboy, two close friends, communicate without necessarily relying on words. They both flee and hide in a church after Johnny kills a rival gang member in self-defense. Subsequently, Johnny dies from injuries resulting from heroic efforts to rescue children from a fire in the church. After Johnny's death, Ponyboy reads a letter from him. This letter reminds Ponyboy to preserve his belief in good things, to watch sunsets, to believe that he can do something with his life. Johnny doesn't want to see Ponyboy lose these qualities or develop a jaundiced eye by becoming too hardened by gang wars on the streets. He wants Ponyboy to treasure his good qualities—including hope for change—which make him the unique person he is. With this message from Johnny, Ponyboy renews his commitment to improving the quality of his life.

Ponyboy also develops a friendship with a young woman named Cherry. Her boyfriend is a member of the rival Socs gang. Ponyboy and Cherry discover how they can talk to each other in a way that they never do with others. As they walk together, Cherry describes to Ponyboy how the Soc gang places so much emphasis on being suave that people lose track of their feelings or search endlessly for contentment. There are times when she finds herself saying something totally opposite to her true feelings:

> You know, sometimes I'll catch myself talking to a girl-friend, and realize I don't mean half of what I'm saying. I don't really think a beer blast on the river bottom is supercool, but I'll rave about one to a girl-friend just to be saying something. (35)

Both Ponyboy and Cherry verbalize honest feelings that would have gone undiscovered if their friendship had not developed.

We're on the Same Wavelength

As young adult literature illustrates, friends can understand each other in ways that other people don't. In Lois Lowry's *A Summer to Die* (1977), Meg, who is thirteen, becomes friends with an older man named Will. They collaborate as Meg teaches Will about photography. Will also shares his knowledge about wild flowers. One day, as they share their excitement over Meg's excellent photography, she notes "... something inside me welled up like hot fudge sauce—sweet, and warm, and so rich that you can't bear to have very much. It was because someone who was a real friend was having the exact same feeling I was having, about something that was more important to me than anything else" (53).

Psychological studies reveal that boys can express their closeness with friends through joint activities (Atwater 1992, 159). In Bruce Brooks' *The Moves Make the Man* (1984), Jerome and Bix develop their friendship as they play basketball, even communicating without words. As Jerome notes:

> Lots of people would say this was nothing to come to love a person over, this silent basketball stuff. You are only supposed to love people over big deals, not just the way he twists with a ball in his hands and watches while you do it a little differently. But I started to think these people were wrong. Anything that could get your heart to where Bix and I were must count as much as anything else. Or at least I thought so then. (155)

The Moves Make the Man also illustrates adolescents' appreciation for the complexity of friendships and for how it takes time to know a friend. Jerome tries to help Bix learn about how to make basketball moves that aren't so literal. After Jerome witnesses Bix's unusual concern about any form of deception or lying, he begins to see how complex their friendship is:

> I still drew to him even at the same time I was set back and watched like he was a stranger or creature, full of a new surprise. Something there I felt like I knew even when I could not see it, something in him that maybe nobody but me recognized. I had never felt most of the things I watched Bix feel, so it was not that I understood everything, for I didn't. It was not that I knew what was coming for him, or what mysteries were in back of him, for I did not, and even when I saw the mysteries revealed I was still mystified. (204)

The complexity of this friendship and others in young adult fiction reminds us that when we are open, there is room for unpredictability and change in our relationships.

Walking a Tightrope: How Much Can I Say?

Young adult fiction mirrors the focus upon self-disclosure in adolescent friendships. Initially, protagonists carefully weigh the pros and cons of concealing or disclosing information. In Sue Ellen Bridgers' *All Together Now* (1979), Casey hides the fact that she is a girl from her friend Dwayne, who is mentally retarded and does not like girls. An older friend named Gwen tells Casey, "One thing I've learned, Casey, . . . Don't ever make a person you care about have to choose between you and something else. Not if you can help it. Don't ever use yourself to bargain with." Reflecting on this, Casey

> knew not telling Dwayne she was a girl kept him from having to choose. She'd performed an act of kindness. That was what she'd thought. That was what she wanted it to be. But was it? Shouldn't she have taken the risk then, before they mattered so much to each other? (175)

Eventually, Dwayne discovers that Casey is a girl. Their friendship does not dissolve, however, because they have a long history of trust and respect.

Finding Out Who Your Friends Really Are

We may not always be able to identify the qualities of healthy interpersonal relationships because some of the most valuable aspects are intangible. Young adult literature portrays adolescents' evolving understanding of what true friendship entails. Tests of character occur when adolescents compete, experience a crises, lose, succeed, or change. Voigt's *Izzy, Willy-Nilly* (1986) illustrates how young people discover who their friends really are.

In this novel, the protagonist, Izzy, has a serious car accident involving a drunken driver. Izzy's leg is amputated as a result of the accident, and she recognizes that her former circle of friends do not really care about her well-being. They gradually stop coming to visit her or only come when a parent pressures them. One friend, Suzy, is more interested in making sure that Izzy does not tell the police that the driver of the car in which Izzy was riding was drunk. This realization hurts Izzy but ultimately leads her to discover more fullfilling relationships.

Rosamunde, who is not popular or attractive by cultural definitions of beauty or by cheerleader standards, is one person who shows up at the hospital and is genuinely interested in Izzy's welfare. As Izzy discovers, Rosamunde is intelligent and nonconventional. Through her direct questions, Rosamunde enables Izzy to confront what has happened to her and deal more openly with her anger and resentment. Izzy also begins to look more carefully at people and recognizes that things are not always as they appear. With Rosamunde's help, Izzy eventually summons the courage to return to school. Similarly, Izzy enables Rosamunde to recognize her own strengths and encourages her to work on self-improvement.

In Chris Crutcher's *Running Loose* (1983), Louie Banks also appreciates his friend Carter, who is loyal even when they disagree. As Louie says:

> [Carter is] one of the most constant things in my life. Doesn't always back my position, but he never tries to take it away from me either. It's one thing to have adults helping you out and giving you direction, but it's another to have someone like Carter who's going through a lot of the same things you are and holding it together with some style. (170–171)

Carter is a faithful friend even after Louie quits the football team because of one coach's unethical behavior.

Cliques and Crowds

In addition to friendships, cliques and crowds play a central role in adolescents' peer relationships. Psychologists now describe different functions of these two groups. Crowds earn reputations and have relatively stronger impact on adolescents' identity development and self-definitions. Cliques are smaller and more instrumental for adolescents' social skills and friendships (Steinberg 1993, 170). Changes in the composition of cliques and crowds from early to late adolescence enable young people to become more adept in their relationships with the opposite sex (Cobb 1995, 272–274).

In Richard Peck's *Remembering The Good Times* (1985), one of the protagonists, Buck, appraises the various types of groups in his high school:

> All these new kids were suddenly in school, and a percentage of them looked like they'd come out of the audience for Saturday Night Live. The Subs were still maintaining their position and their Izod-and-L.L. Bean image. On a clear day you could still make out a few authentic Slos, the polyester people. But now we had punk. We had funk. We had New Wave. We had Culture Club. We had some people walking around who looked like they'd been thrown out of a Billy Idol concert. (76–77)

The protagonist of Hadley Irwin's *Abby, My Love* (1985) describes the norms of his own clique. Members of this tight-knit group

> had only one rule: NO GIRLS! . . . And that's how the MP Club got started, MP for Man Power. We didn't hold meetings or anything like that, but we had a secret sign; a clenched fist and a quick brush at a fellow MP's chin. We kept our membership at five. . . . We adopted tee shirts, blue jeans, and dirty sneakers as our uniforms and let our hair grow. . . . Studying was for stupes. Books for wimps. Baths for babies. Girls for committees. (23, 24)

Group norms fluctuate from one generation to another. What does not change is how important it is for adolescents to decipher the norms and abide by these spoken and unspoken rules. Maureen Daly's *Seventeenth Summer*, published in the 1940s, describes the power of group codes. The protagonist, Angie, notes:

> There was the usual crowd standing in front of the drugstore when we went in. . . . These are the "checkers." They are the more popular crowd at high school and every evening about half-past seven they gather to stand talking together with elaborate unconcern, while in actuality they are sharply watching the cars going by to see what fellows and girls are out together; they watch to see who is having a Coke with whom and to report any violations on the part of the girls who are supposed to be going steady.
>
> It is almost like a secret police system—no one escapes being checked on. At least no one who counts. (91)

Young people's tendency to label and categorize others is pronounced during early adolescence (Pipher 1994, 59).

Conformity to Peers

Research in adolescent psychology indicates that, in general, conformity to the peer group is strongest in early adolescence. During middle and late adolescence, it declines (Cobb 1995, 280–282). Teenagers

are most likely to comply with friends who promote socially unacceptable acts during the ninth grade or at approximately fifteen years
of age (Berndt and Savin-Williams 1993, 207). Recent studies indicate
that although young people can perceive conflicting pressures, parents and peers often share similar values. Adolescents also weigh
input from many different sources rather than rely exclusively on
friends or parents (Sprinthall and Collins 1995, 309, 315).

There are a variety of reasons that conformity to peers is strong
during early adolescence. Young people may temporarily immerse
themselves in a peer group in order to separate from family. They
experiment with different activities, norms, and fads of the clan as a
temporary identity (Muuss 1988, 71). Constant comparison to peers
also stems partially from adolescents' belief in the "imaginary audience." As David Elkind (1981) explains, this belief means that adolescents feel as if they are on stage.

Family relationships also influence adolescents' conformity to
peers. Adolescents raised in permissive or authoritarian homes are
more vulnerable to deviant peer influence. Adolescents who have
close relationships with parents in authoritative homes develop social
competence and are better able to resist peer pressure.

Adolescents' need for social approval is vividly portrayed in Bette
Greene's *The Drowning of Stephan Jones* (1991). In this novel, the
female protagonist, Carla, describes to her mother how important it is
to belong to her peer group, although there is a cost. She explains,

> I don't want to be like you, Mother. I want everybody to like me! So
> what if once in a while I have to pretend to like people I don't like
> or pretend to dislike people that I really like. What's the big deal? It's
> just that simple: I want to be liked. (48)

Eventually, this young woman faces a conflict of values. Carla's
mother has a positive influence on her daughter's moral decisions. At
home, Carla and her mom discuss religion and the church's treatment
of homosexuality. Carla's mother explains how she slowly learned to
stand up for her beliefs and is outraged at the church's hypocrisy as it
preaches love but endorses hatred of homosexuals. This conversation
impresses Carla. Later, when her test of honor arises, Carla stands up
for her beliefs as well, although she loses peer approval.

Wolff's *Make Lemonade* (1993) also shows how the influence of
parents and peers complement each other. In this novel, LaVaughn's
mother initially disapproves of her daughter's commitment to babysit-
ting for Jolly, although she does not prohibit her from keeping the
job. LaVaughn's mother is worried that LaVaughn will get sidetracked
from her studies. Yet LaVaughn sticks to her commitment and also
manages her work at school. She likes helping Jolly with chores and
loves the children. With LaVaughn's help, Jolly changes and no

longer leads such a chaotic life. LaVaughn's mother also learns more about people through her daughter's friendship with Jolly. Previously, she perceived that Jolly was lazy and irresponsible. But when LaVaughn tells her mother about how Jolly saved her own daughter's life, her mother recognizes that she underestimated Jolly's courage and stamina.

Intimidation: I Must Go Along OR ELSE

Even adolescents who are raised in authoritative homes will witness or experience attempts by people to intimidate teens and adults into silence, submission, or crime. Teachers, parents, and adolescents contend with the influence of gangs. Intimidation and mob violence are major themes in young adult literature as well. Examining these topics may help individuals recognize how subtle coercion or manipulation can be. It might happen without people being aware of it, but the impact can be damaging and overpowering.

In several stories, the gang leaders such as Archie in *The Chocolate War* (Cormier 1974) and Andy Harris in *The Drowning of Stephan Jones* (Greene 1991) are cruel, perform malicious pranks, and gain power over others through intimidation. They are shrewd enough to detect what makes other people vulnerable and use this knowledge to take advantage of others. Several adolescents obey gang members because they fear retaliation.

Young adult literature also portrays how adolescents' succumb to adults' misuse of power. A female teacher influences a tight-knit clan in Lois Duncan's *Daughters of Eve* (1979). Irene Stark, the faculty advisor for the exclusive girls' club at Modesta High School, deliberately sways the young women to hate men or turn against their families and other faculty. This cult mesmerizes the girls and they become increasingly isolated from the community. Some young women are drawn to the club because of the problems they face at home. Others feel excluded until they join. Several members have parents who desperately want their daughters to be popular and dating.

In this novel, one female, Tammy Carncross, has a premonition that terrible events will occur. She joins the club but eventually quits and stands up to Irene Stark. She faces a crisis of conscience after the girls in the club physically attack a boy. She recalls the night of violence and acknowledges why she went along. "I wasn't there, not really. Well, yes—yes, I was—but it wasn't because I wanted to be. It was the vote. The majority ruled. I had to go along with that, didn't I?" (195). Eventually Tammy is able to trust her own beliefs. Ann, another member of the club, envies Tammy's independence and courage. After Tammy quits and Ann faces a difficult moral decision of her own, she says aloud to one of the club members, "I'm not like Tammy . . . I wish I were. Tammy has feelings she can trust" (235). Another young woman, Jane Rheardon, is so influenced by the club's violence that she eventually explodes with anger, attacking her father who has physically beaten her mother on many occasions. In a tragic series of events, this violence brings more damage and she becomes a patient in a state mental hospital.

Women also intimidate other women. In Linda Crew's *Children of the River* (1989), one of the protagonists in this novel is Sundara, who arrives in the United States from Cambodia. She gradually understands American norms more clearly and becomes less shy while attending high school in Oregon. Cathy, a cheerleader, will do anything to keep her boyfriend, Jonathan. She warns Sundara to stay away from Jonathan, even though he is attracted to Sundara and wants to date her. Eventually, Sundara becomes more assertive and is no longer afraid of Cathy. When a backlash occurs, Sundara is able to stand by her convictions because she has a clearer sense of her own identity.

Conclusion

Exploring the complex reasons behind intimidation in literature and psychology offers opportunities for people to devise more useful strategies for resisting peer pressure. By examining the significant influence of peers on adolescents and adults, individuals can develop more realistic concepts of intimacy and conformity. The peer pressures among and between adults/parents is not as blatant as what can be discerned more easily among adolescents. Although these forces are more subtle, they are powerful. Peer relations provide a microcosm and testing ground for counteracting social stress.

Works Cited

Alvine, L. 1994. "Understanding Adolescent Homophobia: An Interview with Bette Greene." *The Alan Review* 21(2): 5–9.

Atwater, E. 1992. *Adolescence.* 3d ed. Englewood Cliffs, NJ: Prentice Hall.

Berk, L. E. 1993. *Infants, Children, and Adolescents.* Boston: Allyn & Bacon.

Berndt, T. J., and R. C. Savin-Williams. 1993. "Peer Relationships and Friendships." In *Handbook of Clinical Research and Practice with Adolescents,* edited by P. H. Tolan and B. Cohler, 203–219. New York: John Wiley & Sons.

Bridgers, S. E. 1979. *All Together Now.* New York: Alfred A. Knopf.

Brooks, B. 1984. *The Moves Make the Man.* New York: HarperKeypoint.

Cobb, N. J. 1995. *Adolescence: Continuity, Change, and Diversity.* 2d ed. Mountain View, CA: Mayfield.

Cormier, R. 1974. *The Chocolate War.* New York: Dell.

Crew, L. 1989. *Children of the River.* New York: Dell.

Crutcher, C. 1983. *Running Loose.* New York: Dell.

Daly, M. 1942. *Seventeenth Summer.* New York: Dodd, Mead & Company.

Duncan, L. 1979. *Daughters of Eve.* New York: Dell.

Elkind, D. 1981. *The Hurried Child: Growing Up Too Fast Too Soon.* Reading, MA: Addison-Wesley.

Greene, B. 1991. *The Drowning of Stephan Jones.* New York: Bantam Books.

Hadley, L., and A. Irwin. 1985. *Abby, My Love.* New York: Atheneum.

Hinton, S. E. 1967. *The Outsiders.* New York: Dell.

Kimmel, D. C., and I. Weiner. 1995. *Adolescence: A Developmental Transition.* 2d ed. New York: John Wiley & Sons.

Lowry, L. 1977. *A Summer to Die.* New York: Dell.

Muuss, R. E. 1988. *Theories of Adolescence.* 5th ed. New York: Random House.

Peck, R. 1985. *Remembering the Good Times.* New York: Dell.

Pipher, M. 1994. *Reviving Ophelia: Saving the Selves of Adolescent Girls.* New York: Ballantine Books.

Santrock, J. W. 1996. *Adolescence: An Introduction.* 6th ed. Madison, WI: Brown & Benchmark.

Sprinthall, N. A., and W. A. Collins. 1995. *Adolescent Psychology: A Developmental View.* 3d ed. New York: McGraw-Hill.

Steinberg, L. 1993. *Adolescence.* 3d ed. New York: McGraw-Hill.

Steinberg, L., and A. Levine. 1990. *You and Your Adolescent: A Parent's Guide for Ages Ten to Twenty.* New York: Harper & Row.

Voigt, C. 1986. *Izzy, Willy-Nilly.* New York: Aladdin Paperbacks.

Wolff, V. E. 1993. *Make Lemonade.* New York: Scholastic.

Woodson, J. 1994. *I Hadn't Meant to Tell You This.* New York: Bantam Doubleday Dell Books.

Four

There's a War Going on Inside My Head

Too often the conflicts in our heads prevent us from reaching our full potential. It is easy to underestimate the power of our interior monologues and focus instead on our behaviors; we often believe that tangible acts are the only proof of change. However, significant modification also requires thinking through our behaviors.

How and what we think, as well as our interior monologues, have a dramatic influence on our interpretation of events and on our behaviors. Our version of reality is strongly based on our viewing angle. We recognize that everybody's perspective about their inner and outer worlds can differ. Throughout life, we can sharpen our outlooks in order to be more accurate. The tools we need to do so include cognitive skills, emotional development, and outside experience. Psychologists emphasize that adolescence is not a period of "storm and stress." Yet, like us, teenagers face important conflicts. Any clash inside the head influences the connection between thought and action. It can reflect the struggle to gain psychological strength as teenagers try to become their own persons. There will be better linkage between thinking and action when they resolve the battle.

Psychological studies and young adult literature illustrate how the war inside the head can be resolved as we become better able to decipher reality and understand that things aren't always what they appear to be. This insight contributes to psychological vitality. As individuals confront interior enemies, they can resolve the battles in their outside world. We cannot read minds and resolve the inner conflicts of other people. Yet teachers who help their students better understand their own thought processes play a very valuable role.

If we learn to appreciate the distinction between appearance and reality, we become less vulnerable to the myth that psychological growth is synonymous with effortless action and quick change. Mental acumen lessens our tendency to judge ourselves only by looking at our own or other people's exterior. These comparisons hamper change. As the interior battle is won, individuals reach a strong conviction about what they are capable of doing, and this certainty energizes actions.

Young adult literature describes how the interior monologue can lead to constructive change. In turn, readers better appreciate that things aren't always what they appear to be. With this genre, we go inside the head and notice discrepancies between thought and action. We also discover the sources of cohesion between thinking and action. This inside view enables us to dismiss glamorous, idealized versions of change and freedom.

Just Do It: The Myth About Psychological Freedom

If only we could sprint quickly and do all things according to the Nike commercial that advocates "just do it." Like adolescents, we are often impatient for signs of change and accept a fallacy that psychological stamina simply entails doing things automatically without struggle. Healthy progress requires effort and courage. Such change draws more authenticity when it is hard won. Many adolescents feel pressure to do something because their peers tell them that they are too inhibited. By giving in, many hope to feel sturdy, but just the opposite can occur.

Oddballs, Sleepwalkers, and Spies: What Is Happening to Me?

Like the protagonists of young adult literature, each of us can feel like an oddball who is different from everyone else, a sleepwalker who is motionless, and a spy who searches for answers to mysteries. These roles parallel the sense of orphanhood discussed in Chapter 2. The innocence and endurance of these newcomers to adolescence are startling to the outside observer. I have heard it said that adolescence is similar to landing abruptly in a foreign territory. No one is certain of the customs or the language, both of which seem to change continually.

I Feel Like the Oddball

Often, the characters in young adult literature feel as if some experience sets them apart from others. They may search for ways that they can become like everybody else and not feel so different. The wars inside their heads center on finding ways that they can fit into this new territory and still be true to themselves.

Feeling like "the oddball" in young adult literature coincides with David Elkind's description of adolescent egocentrism (1981, 112–115). This link enhances our understanding of protagonists such as Carrie in Zibby Oneal's *The Language of Goldfish* (1990) and others who have a difficult transition during adolescence. Although talented in math and art, Carrie becomes increasingly alienated from her family and peers as she faces new maturity demands. Carrie wonders if finding a niche was easier for other people. As she explains to her art teacher, she feels like the only person who does not fit into place.

In Elizabeth Speare's *The Witch of Blackbird Pond* (1958), the protagonist, Kit, also feels like an alien. After her grandfather dies, she travels by ship from Barbados in order to find a home with her aunt and uncle in Connecticut. As she begins her life in their home, she has difficulty understanding their strict customs and spartan life. The people in town think Kit is strange. She jumps into the water and swims in order to rescue a little girl's doll. Her rescue efforts and ability to swim are greeted with disdain. She is often reprimanded for her free spirit and unconventional ways. A friend named Nat tells Kit that he always knew she was different from people in the community. He expresses his wish that she not lose her lively spirit. Both Carrie and Kit eventually find their place without becoming listless. They both develop a firmer sense of who they are and remain true to their identity.

I'm Sleepwalking Through Life

Young adult literature also includes stories about protagonists who feel as if they are sleepwalking through life. Until they change, they are frustrated and recognize that they are not doing anything heartfelt or meaningful. Often, an internal part of them seems closed off or asleep. Inside their heads, they sense the gap between thought and action. Their heads tell them one thing, their emotions and actions another. They also recognize the discrepancy between their idealism and their actions in everyday life.

This war resembles psychologists' distinction between early and late formal operational thinking. During early formal operations, adolescents consider what is possible but have initial difficulty putting their idealistic notions into practice. In contrast, during late formal operations, adolescents become more realistic in their problem solving and can better implement thinking into action (Santrock 1996, 109).

No matter how bright the person, intellectual knowledge alone is not sufficient for instigating change. Protagonists of young adult literature tell us, it's one thing to know something, it's another thing to do it. As the saying goes, "You can talk the talk but can you walk the walk?" Psychological insight, like good literature, is most compelling when it strikes deep, involving our emotions. Without this depth, it is not possible to attain freedom or compassion. The sleepwalkers' challenge is learning new connections between their thinking and emotions.

For example, in Terry Davis' *If Rock and Roll Were a Machine* (1992), Bert Bowden decides to buy a motorcycle. His parents protest because they are afraid that he could be hurt in a crash. They don't want to see him injured or worse on the roadside after an accident. Bert, who feels like he really isn't doing anything, replies that he already feels like a vegetable. His personal awakening includes learning how to win dignity by doing the one thing that he knows he has always wanted—to become an excellent athlete.

Chap Reaver's *A Little Bit Dead* (1992) illustrates how someone who is less vibrant becomes more enlivened. In this novel, the protagonist, Reece, saves a Native American named Shanti from being lynched by a group of greedy, corrupt men. Reece and Shanti become friends, travel together, and describe their histories to each other. Later, several men who had tried to hang Shanti accuse Reece of murder. Reece has to prove that he is innocent. Shanti offers spiritual guidance and assistance to Reece. His advice prevents Reece from resorting to cowardice for revenge against his enemies. As Reece meets this challenge, a part of him that had died with his father's death reawakens. Many times during his ordeal, he recalls his father's words about the importance of trying to do the right thing. Through his friendship and journey with Shanti, Reece becomes more connected to an important part of himself that had been buried.

I Am a Spy

The spies of young adult literature are searching for answers to a mystery. The war inside their head begins with a discovery that things aren't always what they appear to be. This insight offers important clues that they have to dig deeper in order to find out just what reality is rather than rely on appearance alone. Distinguishing between appearance and reality reduces the psychological warfare inside their heads and offers escape. Spies in young adult literature remind me of psychologists' descriptions of how adolescents can hide their accomplishments or pretend to know less than they do in order to avoid conflict or escape peer rejection (Gilligan 1990, 14; Pipher 1994, 63–64).

In Robert Cormier's novels *I Am the Cheese* (1977), *Fade* (1988), and *The Bumblebee Flies Anyway* (1983), protagonists become spies and watch people who they suspect may have a hidden agenda. These spies disguise their feelings or hide how much they know in order to escape the psychological mind game induced by others. For example, in *The Bumblebee Flies Anyway,* Barney Snow constantly debates exactly how much to say to other people as he begins to solve a mystery about what is happening to him. This story describes how young people cope as subjects of memory experiments at an institution. Barney always believes that he is not terminally ill like the other patients until he discovers more details about his own victimization. He tries to hide knowledge and discoveries from a doctor (the Handyman) who conducts the experiments. A chilling cat-and-mouse game unfolds. Barney masterminds a final flight to freedom for one of the other patients.

The Wheels Are Turning Inside My Head

Psychologists frequently refer to the work of Jean Piaget and David Elkind (1981) to describe what goes on inside the heads of adolescents. According to Piaget, the fourth stage of cognitive development, labeled *Formal Operations,* begins at approximately eleven or twelve years of age. Not all individuals attain this stage of cognitive development, and individuals may display Formal Operational thinking in some areas but not in others.

The new cognitive skills of Formal Operations include abstract thinking (the ability to consider unseen events); introspection (to turn one's thoughts inward); reasoning about the hypothetical; idealism; and metacognition (thinking about one's own thinking). Both metacognition and introspection contribute to adolescents' increased self-awareness and reflection. Adolescents are also capable of using deductive logic (reasoning from the general to the particular), which enhances scientific problem solving during this stage. Formal Operational thinking also enables people to understand that individuals can view the same situation from different perspectives. Adolescents evaluate these multiple points of view with much more skill than children. As a result, they can understand and integrate different sides of their own self-concepts and others' personalities (Cobb 1995, 156–163; Sprinthall and Collins 1995, 98–109; Steinberg 1993, 58–69).

These cognitive skills influence every aspect of adolescents' lives, including morality, identity development, and self-understanding. Answers to the question "Who am I?" take on new meaning when individuals look beneath the surface and think about their own thinking. The new analytical skills of adolescents can lead to intense self-scrutiny and self-consciousness. At times, teenagers may analyze situations and people in minute detail. They can also focus on "doing" acts in order to avoid self-reflection; extremes of overactivity can be a symptom of depression when adolescents are very troubled and do not want time to think (Atwater 1992, 366; Kimmel and Weiner 1995, 522). Resolving self-doubts and conflicts depends on using new cognitive skills to better decipher reality.

Young people can analyze motives, study people, and appreciate different perspectives as they filter experiences through new cognitive lenses. They can also temporarily exaggerate or distort individuals' views of people or events. These biases resemble David Elkind's concepts of adolescents' egocentrism and pseudostupidity.

As Elkind (1981, 112–115) explains, adolescent egocentrism includes the personal fable and the imaginary audience (adolescents' feelings of being on stage). Teenagers' self-consciousness, reluctance to disclose information about themselves, and increased need for privacy can stem from a belief in the imaginary audience. The imaginary audience increases young people's sense that everyone is watching them intently.

Elkind also describes another quality of thinking labeled *pseudostupidity* (Rice 1996, 152). It refers to adolescents' tendency to overanalyze people or make situations more complicated than they are. He emphasizes that adolescents are mentally sharp but need more experience implementing their newfound cognitive skills.

I'm Holding on to My Dreams

Another new quality of teenagers' thinking is idealism and the ability to consider the hypothetical. These skills can be a valuable instigator of change, providing determination and belief in the capacity for self-enhancement. It can also lead people to overinvest in dreams or to become very critical. Although idealism adds many benefits, it can instigate conflicts inside the head. For example, individuals might perceive a gap between their ideal and real selves or notice the discrepancy between their thinking and action. Adolescents' coming of age includes learning how to blend idealism with realistic action and problem solving.

In Davis' *If Rock and Roll Were a Machine* (1992), Bert Bowden's description of "Bowdenland" reflects idealism. Bert visualizes Bowdenland as a fantasy place where he reaches stardom, with a crowd watching him ride his new Harley Davidson motorcycle with a girl as his companion. Hadley Irwin's *Abby, My Love* (1985) provides another example of idealism. The protagonist, Chip Martin, has just purchased his own automobile. As he drives the car with Abby, the girl he has had a crush on since the age of thirteen, he idealistically imagines the audience:

> Just for a minute, I had a picture in my head from one of those dumb teen-age movies—the kind where this handsome guy and this beautiful girl sort of whip into the drive-in in this long, low convertible and all of a sudden everyone is singing and dancing all over the parking lot in Technicolor and stereophonic sound. (94)

His brief moment of imagination releases him from the ordinary.

My Victory Cry: My Mind Is Made Up

The friction inside the head partially mirrors individuals' struggle for self-actualization. Until the internal conflicts are resolved, however, we reenact them in our outside world. People who win the war recognize their own inside enemies of fear, anger, or envy. They also see the outside world more accurately. The most important achievement is reaching a strong internal conviction. This certainty helps individuals tackle demanding challenges.

For example, protagonists discover that jealousy, which has prevented them from reaching their full potential, can be reduced by channeling their energy into becoming who they are rather than by fighting others. They gradually recognize how they are their own worst enemy. In Katherine Paterson's *Jacob Have I Loved* (1980), the protagonist, Louise, feels jealous of her talented twin sister, Caroline, who is adored by everyone. Louise eventually recognizes that she too can become whatever she aspires to be. She sorts through her complicated feelings and discovers that any obstacles holding her back exist primarily inside herself. Forming her own identity, she leaves home, studies to become a midwife, and eventually marries.

Chris Crutcher's *Chinese Handcuffs* (1989) describes the effects of battles inside the head. In this novel, a coach helps a young person to develop a new approach to handling difficult situations. At one point, Dillon, the protagonist, feels like his life is turbulent. As the coach points out, Dillon's most dramatic battles exist inside his head, not in the outside world. He has no control over other people's reactions, but he can take charge of his own life. After talking to his coach, Dillon begins to rechannel his energy and focuses on constructive change instead of constantly fighting outside adversaries.

We also witness protagonists' struggles between good and evil. This battle mirrors efforts to maintain psychological integrity as well.

In literature and life, crime may haunt or imprison youth. In Cormier's *Fade* (1988), once the protagonist, Paul, recognizes his special skill to become invisible, he struggles with the temptation to use this hidden talent for good or evil purposes. He can observe and eavesdrop on people who do not know that he is there. After Paul murders a corrupt man for revenge, he vows to never use his ability to become invisible again. Yet his conflict between good and evil does not disappear until it is fully resolved. Paul eventually faces a confrontation in his outer world with his nephew Ozzie. Their duel represents the conflict between good and evil in the outside world.

Katherine Paterson's *Lyddie* (1991) illustrates how a young woman reaches a strong internal belief when she resolves her conflict between freedom and oppression. Set in the 1800s, this story begins with the protagonist, Lyddie, and her family confronting a bear who enters their home in search of food. They escape the bear, which eventually flees. The animal symbolizes the internal conflicts that Lyddie faces during her struggles. The mother and the siblings are forced to separate and live apart in order to survive. Lyddie leaves home and begins to work long hours in a mill in order to support her family. She hopes to earn enough money to bring everyone back together. However, events turn out differently from what Lyddie originally expects. This brave woman eventually faces a decision about whether or not to sign a petition with other women at work about unfair working conditions. As she helps defend another female at the mill from the overseer, Lyddie has a vivid image inside her head of the bear. Ultimately, Lyddie is fired from her job in the mills, yet this change does not guarantee her new freedom. She finally stands up against the boss who fires her. Soon after, Lyddie can focus on her own welfare. She resolves "to stare down the bear" inside herself so that she can achieve whatever future goals she sets (181).

I Know Who I Am Now

People who have a difficult passage yet work hard to resolve conflicts can reach a more complete sense of self. Carefully weighing the consequences of choices and surviving life crises may catalyze individuals to realize what is important to them. Meeting an unusual person can also trigger insights.

In Speare's *The Witch of Blackbird Pond* (1958), one character, John Holbrook, travels to New England on the same ship as the protagonist, Kit. They became friends during the journey. Both begin a new life in Connecticut. After settling into the community, Kit notices that John does not seem to be the same person she had come to know during their voyage. Preparing to be a minister, he is devoted to his studies. Yet, somehow, he seems to have buried a part of himself by accepting without any disagreement everything that his teacher believes. Eventually, however, John does change. He respects his teacher, but decides that he cannot agree with everything that this mentor believes. Once John's mind is made up, he becomes more true to his own beliefs instead of remaining silent.

Gary Paulsen's *Sentries* (1986) describes a similar tranformation. A young woman, Sue, meets a Native American named Alan. He is unlike anyone she has ever met. She is baffled and intrigued by him. As she spends time with this man, Sue begins to change, listening much more closely to her grandfather's talk. Before, she had always dismissed his stories and conversations as false and meaningless. Through Alan, Sue becomes more alive, looking and listening more carefully to the people in her life. She recognizes that she will never be the same person.

Telling It Like It Is

Attaining a stronger sense of self, individuals in literature and life also replace deep cynicism or bitter disillusionment with a sharper perspective about what really counts. This reappraisal summons realistic problem solving. Young adult literature offers constructive examples of how adolescents and adults interpret their experiences more accurately. In Will Hobbs' *Changes in Latitudes* (1988), a vacation for a mother, her two sons, and daughter is planned as an idyllic escape. It is not peaceful, and the youngest boy dies unexpectedly. Initially, the family is fragmented. Each person is self-absorbed and goes his or her own way. The father does not accompany the family on their vacation. After the tragic loss, however, the siblings and parents recognize that they have not been available to each other. The oldest son reaches out to his mother to remind her that they have to help each other. The family pulls together. They no longer bury their problems through escape.

Robert Lipsyte's *The Contender* (1967) provides an excellent example of how a young person becomes more realistic about tenacity. Living in Harlem, a young man named Alfred Brooks has quit school and wants to become a champion boxer. At the beginning of his training, a coach named Donatelli guides him with the following advice:

> Everybody wants to be a champion. That's not enough. You have to start by wanting to be a contender, the man coming up, the man who knows there's a good chance he'll never get to the top, the man who's

willing to sweat and bleed to get up as high as his legs and his brains
and his heart will take him. That must sound corny to you. (27)

Alfred discovers that becoming an exceptional fighter has less to do
with winning and much more to do with perseverance. It involves
small victories too. For example, Alfred knows he takes a step forward
when he is able to resist peer pressure to rob the store where he
works. However, it is not just a smooth ride after this success. He
backtracks temporarily. To his credit, Alfred returns to the gym and
begins training again. This young man gains dignity and it affects
every aspect of his life in positive ways.

Conclusion

As many protagonists illustrate, internal change provides more connection between thinking and action. This hinge resolves the discrepancy between the ideal and the real self. Like us, when protagonists
set more realistic goals and become better able to carry them out, they
gain self-confidence and pride. The connection between thinking and
action is real!

Works Cited

Atwater, E. 1992. *Adolescence*. 3d ed. Englewood Cliffs, NJ: Prentice-Hall.

Avi. 1990. *The True Confessions of Charlotte Doyle*. New York: Avon.

Cobb, N. J. 1995. *Adolescence: Continuity, Change, and Diversity*. 2d ed. Mountain
    View, CA: Mayfield.

Cormier, R. 1977. *I Am the Cheese*. New York: Dell.

————. 1983. *The Bumblebee Flies Anyway*. New York: Dell.

————. 1988. *Fade*. New York: Dell.

Crutcher, C. 1989. *Chinese Handcuffs*. New York: Dell.

Davis, T. 1992. *If Rock and Roll Were a Machine*. New York: Bantam Doubleday
    Dell Books.

Elkind, D. 1981. *The Hurried Child: Growing Up Too Fast Too Soon*. Reading, MA:
    Addison-Wesley.

Gilligan, C. 1990. "Teaching Shakespeare's Sister: Notes from the Under-
    ground of Female Adolescence." In *Making Connections: The Relational
    Worlds of Adolescent Girls at Emma Willard School*, edited by C. Gilligan,
    N. P. Lyons, and T. J. Hanmer, 6–29. Cambridge, MA: Harvard University
    Press.

Hadley, L., and A. Irwin. 1985. *Abby, My Love*. New York: Atheneum.

Hobbs, W. 1988. *Changes in Latitudes*. New York: Avon Books.

Kimmel, D. C., and I. Weiner. 1995. *Adolescence: A Developmental Transition.* 2d ed. New York: John Wiley & Sons.

Lipsyte, R. 1967. *The Contender.* New York: HarperCollins.

Oneal, Z. 1990. *The Language of Goldfish.* New York: Puffin Books.

Paterson, K. 1980. *Jacob Have I Loved.* New York: HarperKeypoint.

———. 1991. *Lyddie.* New York: Puffin.

Paulsen, G. 1986. *Sentries.* New York: Puffin.

Pipher, M. 1994. *Reviving Ophelia: Saving the Selves of Adolescent Girls.* New York: Ballantine Books.

Reaver, C. 1992. *A Little Bit Dead.* Bantam Doubleday Dell Books.

Rice, F. P. 1996. *The Adolescent: Development, Relationships and Culture.* 8th ed. Boston: Allyn & Bacon.

Santrock, J. 1996. *Adolescence: An Introduction.* 6th ed. Madison, WI: Brown & Benchmark.

Speare, E. G. 1958. *The Witch of Blackbird Pond.* New York: Dell.

Sprinthall, N. A., and W. A. Collins. 1995. *Adolescent Psychology: A Developmental View.* 3d ed. New York: McGraw-Hill.

Steinberg, L. 1993. *Adolescence.* 3d ed. New York: McGraw-Hill.

Five

Finding My Niche

Often when we hear a beautiful song, see a memorable painting, or read a powerful book, we pause and think about the source and inspiration for such achievement. All age groups are drawn to authenticity. However, it can seem unattainable to many people. As teachers, how often have we heard students say, "I could never do that"? So much comparison to other people can make us freeze. Our culture often focuses on the tangible signs of success, yet the invisible labor that goes into a product of artistic or scientific merit offers its own immeasurable rewards. Because the final product's simplicity can look effortless, we frequently overlook the intangible benefits of hard work and discipline.

Teachers who enable students to recognize their wide range of talents, work hard, and realize their full potential play an invaluable role. How many of us know one such teacher who made a difference in our lives? Examining intelligence, competition, success, and failure in young adult fiction within the context of psychological studies on adolescent achievement, can help educators, parents, and adolescents find innovative solutions to educational challenges and dilemmas.

Seeing Is Believing

There is much achievement pressure on young people today. They face stiff competition for entry into prestigious schools and well-paying jobs. Adolescents and their families also face financial and social pressures. Our culture habitually focuses on discernible products of success and failure. Moreover, the media promotes visions of instant success. No wonder young people look for quick answers or signs of immediate change. All of us become frustrated when effective, longlasting solutions to complex problems evolve slowly and answers do not appear promptly. Unfortunately, our culture often defines achievement in terms of successes. Yet, we can develop valuable resources as we cope with setbacks, failure, or defeat.

What Psychologists Say About Achievement

One of adolescents' chief anxieties is school performance. Studies in psychology indicate that parents' involvement and authoritative styles of childrearing enhance their adolescents' academic achievement, particularly as their teenagers move from middle school to high school (Melby and Conger 1996, 113–137). In contrast, parental hostility and lack of parental supervision are linked to adolescents' decreased academic performance. Research also indicates that teenagers who work excessive hours in jobs outside the home experience declines in academic motivation and achievement. Psychologists recommend that parents monitor their sons' and daughters' hours of work while attending school (Steinberg and Levine 1990, 344–350).

School environments during early adolescence can affect achievement. The studies of Jacquelynne Eccles (Eccles et al. 1993, 90–101) and other investigators (Dacey and Kenny 1994, 314) link young adults' underachievement to a poor fit between schools' structure and adolescents' developmental needs. The switch from a relatively small, personal elementary school with much individualized attention to an impersonal junior high school with larger classes, less tailored instruction, and more structure, corresponds poorly with the developmental needs of adolescents. The changes introduced in junior high school may also increase young people's comparison to and competitiveness with others. Adolescents' push for autonomy includes wanting increased say in decisions and perhaps less structure, not more. Within this context, decreases in academic performance and motivation occur for young adolescents who face multiple, concurrent changes such as school transitions and puberty (Eccles 1993, 91, citing Simmons and colleagues).

Psychologists also examine differences between men's and women's achievements in math and science. In her text *Adolescence*, Nancy Cobb (1995) reviews the research of Carol Dweck and others on individuals' explanations for success and failure. Studies reveal that men more often attribute their successes to ability and their failure to lack of effort. As a result, they are more likely to persist with difficult tasks. In contrast, women believe that the major causes of their successes include luck, hard work, or the simplicity of tasks. However, they attribute their failure to lack of ability. This pattern of attributions leads women to give up more often after failure than men. Females with high ability are particularly likely to withdraw from difficult, challenging work (Cobb 1995, 311–312).

According to Carol Dweck and other researchers, these differences in explanations for failure can influence women's attitudes toward math. In junior high school, adolescents face more difficult mathematical problems. If females are more likely to give up easily after failure, they in turn may not persist in solving difficult mathematical problems (Cobb 1995, 312).

During early adolescence, females have concerns about dating, popularity, and social acceptance. They can experience conflicting pressures about academic performance and social status, particularly when beginning high school. As they attempt to integrate messages about achievement from peers, school, and parents, young women weigh potential complex effects (Steinberg 1995, 263, 394). I have heard psychologists, parents, and teachers give examples of how adolescent females or gifted youth devalue or hide their talents in order to be accepted by peers (Pipher 1994, 63–64).

Young adult literature provides examples of subtle and overt socialization of women away from challenging academic work. This cultural phenomenon is shifting. However, even parents of adolescent females may undermine their daughter's achievement motivation. Gary Paulsen's novel *Sisters* (1993) depicts the pressure on women to be attractive and fit cultural standards of beauty. In this novel, one mother dominates her daughter's life so much that it resembles a form of prostitution. She coaches her daughter, Traci, to believe that making the cheerleading team, being popular, and looking beautiful are the most essential goals in life because these feats will determine her future prospects for marrying well. In Zibby Oneal's *The Language of Goldfish* (1983), the protagonist, Carrie, has special aptitudes in math and art. She tells her father that one of her classmates has difficulty with math. His response reflects how society can devalue women's academic achievement in comparison to their physical attractiveness: "Well, she's a pretty little girl. She'll never have to understand. Nobody'll ever care whether she can add two and two" (31–32). Statements like this influence young people's achievement in both interpersonal and academic realms.

What Psychologists Say About Intelligence

There is a longstanding debate in psychology about what intelligence is. Intelligence is hard to see, since people do not wear it like caps on their heads. The work of Howard Gardner, Robert Sternberg, and others moves us away from narrow definitions of intelligence that are based on IQ tests or academic grades. Successful job performance and what

Sternberg refers to as "tacit knowledge" are valued by our society (Sternberg 1995, 258). His research adds new emphases to training individuals' practical intelligence as preparation for the competitive job market. Additional studies have also incorporated interpersonal skills, self-understanding, and emotional IQ in definitions of intelligence. Multicultural literature and psychological studies also underline that cultures may not agree on their definitions of intelligence. What might be viewed as astute behavior in one culture may not necessarily be viewed as intelligent in another. Howard Gardner and others do not promote typecasting or stereotyping individuals. Instead, they propose that appreciating different types of intelligence can stimulate innovative teaching in the classroom (Armstrong 1994, 1–35) and prevent us from underestimating people's potential.

These views enrich our understanding of the thoughtful portrayal of protagonists in young adult literature. We are struck by the quiet intelligence of protagonists such as Ponyboy in Susan Hinton's *The Outsiders* (1967) and the quick wit of Gilly Hopkins in Katherine Paterson's *The Great Gilly Hopkins* (1978). Gilly, who relishes driving her teachers crazy, is not alone. In other young adult novels such as Avi's *Nothing But the Truth* (1991) and Paul Zindel's *The Pigman* (1968), protagonists watch or participate to see if the con artist wins or loses. Who comes out on the short end? In Bruce Brooks' *Midnight Hour Encores* (1986), the protagonist, Sibilance, who is a talented musician, observes other students and draws her own conclusions:

> There are some kids who are as clever at playing School as I am at playing the cello. They find their way around all sides of each teacher and each subject with the same kind of cunning and arrogance (to use two of the words that keep following me around in my reviews) that I use to learn a new piece under a big conductor. I like watching them operate, but they don't really teach me anything. (17)

Holding less-narrow views of intelligence, protagonists grow and appreciate the intelligent strengths of other people. For example, in *The Outsiders*, Ponyboy describes his friend Johnny's intelligence. Johnny does not do well in school. But, as Ponyboy recognizes, Johnny derives so much from his experiences because he's always thinking. Similarly, Gilly is startled by the intelligent approach of her teacher, Miss Harris. This is the first teacher Gilly knows who is not rattled easily by her students.

A related theme in young adult literature is that adolescents learn to value their own talents and intelligence rather than to overlook their skills. Some recognize that although they do not do well in school, they are very bright. In Chris Crutcher's *Running Loose* (1983), Louie Banks recognizes that he is smart, even if he does not have high academic grades. He says ". . . I'm no dummy—despite my 2.46 grade point average—I know things can change" (121). Young adult literature does not devalue book smarts. Yet, this genre also includes stories of how people learn to use their intelligence to improve interpersonal relationships (Carl Swaggers of Alden Carter's *Up Country*), gain self-understanding (Charlotte of Avi's *The True Confessions of Charlotte Doyle*), and earn dignity (Bert Bowden of Terry Davis' *If Rock and Roll Were a Machine;* Reece in Chap Reaver's *A Little Bit Dead*). Several protagonists develop specific interests (photography for Meg of Lois Lowry's *A Summer to Die;* music for Neal of Suzanne Newton's *I Will Call It Georgie's Blues* and for Maybeth in Cynthia Voigt's *Homecoming;* art and math for Carrie of Zibby Oneal's *The Language of Goldfish;* writing for Bert of Terry Davis' *If Rock and Roll Were a Machine* and for Lorraine of Paul Zindel's *The Pigman*). Discipline and training help protagonists crystallize their experiences. In turn, some individuals such as Ponyboy of *The Outsiders* hope they can help others by writing about their experiences. In these stories, parents, teachers, and siblings learn to avoid underestimating individuals' talents. In Cynthia Voigt's *Dicey's Song* (1982), Dicey and her brothers meet and become friends with a teacher who nurtures their sister Maybeth's talent in music. Beforehand, adults and others had viewed Maybeth as "slow." Like several protagonists listed above, Maybeth illustrates Howard Gardner's description of musical intelligence.

I Better Not Know More than the Teacher

Teachers have powerful influence on adolescents' views of their intelligence and motivation. Both positive and negative effects of educators are described in young adult literature. In Davis' *If Rock and Roll Were a Machine* (1992), Bert Bowden feels immobilized by one teacher, Gary Lawler. Bert describes how he used to be a really enthusiastic kid who loved to learn but discovered quickly that he could not say too much or Lawler would ridicule him for self-importance. Soon, Bert learned to just shut down in class:

> I thought I understood how a staked dog might feel. Lawler's questions would cruise by like fat newspaper kids on cheap bicycles, and my mind would scramble off after them like a crazed Doberman. I'd get right to the edge of the grass, my sharp little fifth-grader's intellectual fangs all shiny and dripping, poised to rip jeans and sneakers, and then I'd come to the end of the rope. I'd feel it constrict around my throat, and I couldn't shout or speak in a normal tone or even whisper. I just stayed right there at the edge of the sidewalk with my paw in the air ready to be called on. But I never got called on. (49)

One day, Bert expresses his own knowledge and opinion in class during a discussion about fighting in Lebanon. He knows about the topic based on his own reading. Lawler pounces on Bert immediately, ridiculing him for speaking in class. This man informs the other students that they will have to help keep Bert silent. This scenario illustrates how teachers can stifle students' love of learning or make people feel as if they have to apologize for their intelligence.

False Moves

During the psychosocial moratorium (see Chapter 1), adolescents explore different roles. Before they find their niche, they may feel as if they are groping. Anxious or frustrated adolescents may compare themselves too much to their peers or try to be someone they aren't. After experimenting, adolescents can realize that a choice that they have been considering is not what they want to do.

For example, in Brooks' *Midnight Hour Encores* (1986), the protagonist, Sib, is a talented musician who is ranked "about third or fourth" in the world as a cello player (16). At her audition for a prestigious institute, she plays beautifully, but during the end of her performance, she plays an encore that jeopardizes her acceptance. Deep down Sib knows that the academy is not the right fit for her. Sib's decision is partially based upon experimentation with a new lifestyle while staying with her mother and also reflects her realization about what is important to her.

Other protagonists see that they are not enjoying what they do. In Linda Crew's *Children of the River* (1989), Jonathan develops a valuable friendship with Sundara, a young woman from Cambodia. When Sundara describes the hardships that she has experienced, Jonathan begins to reevaluate his own preferences. Gradually, he recognizes that he does not like playing football and that he may be doing it simply to please everybody else. The tough challenge is that the coach and classmates at school are angry and dismayed after Jonathan quits the team. Jonathan knows he has been honest with himself and feels that he has made the right choice. He illustrates a positive outcome of exploration during the psychosocial moratorium.

Competition: The Heat Is On

I'm Training the Right Way

Young adult novels portray the merits of honest discipline and demonstrate how a person can learn to perform better in honest competition. The ingredients for success include minimizing unrealistic comparisons to other people. To illustrate, Crutcher's *Running Loose*

(1983) demonstrates how training for competition can enhance individuals' psychological well-being. Initially, Louie Banks withdraws from athletics after becoming disillusioned with a football coach's dirty tactics. But with the encouragement of another coach, he begins training in track, instead of dropping sports entirely. Louie follows his coach's advice to avoid comparing himself to the other athletes because it creates unnecessary obstacles. In the long term, Louie earns much respect from another talented athlete, who is his competitor, because he trains with honest discipline. This novel illustrates the positive side of competition. Well-trained athletes respect their rivals, and are admired for disciplined integrity.

I'm Hiding

Educators emphasize how important it is to identify and nurture the talents of gifted individuals. They have special educational needs. At some point, the gifted may face a choice to do mediocre work in order to win approval of their peers rather than to perform to the best of their ability (Fuhrmann 1990, 323). All adolescents can face similar pressures. In Voigt's *Dicey's Song* (1982), Dicey's brother James has always performed well in school. He writes a beautiful paper on the Pilgrims that he shares with Dicey. Yet James submits a less-outstanding report to his teacher so that he will not stand out from his peers.

In Newton's *I Will Call It Georgie's Blues* (1983), Neal Sloan conceals his passionate love of music from his family and peers. Neal compartmentalizes different aspects of his life, keeping his family and music lessons separate from one another. Neal believes that if his father discovers his talent, the man will assume control over all of his practicing and training. Then, music would no longer be something that Neal feels is his own. The music teacher, Mrs. T, recognizes this young man's gift and is very supportive. Respecting Neal's needs, she also reminds him that there is a high cost to hiding such an important part of oneself—it takes enormous energy. Neal could use that strength more constructively. Over time, he discovers how much the different aspects of his life interconnect. When he stops concealing, Neal can play music openly in the church with an audience. The music he composes, "Georgie's Blues," is a tribute to his brother Georgie's plea for people to be themselves.

Overall, portrayals in young adult fiction also dispel romantic views that gifted individuals excel without effort. Protagonists such as Carrie of Oneal's *The Language of Goldfish* (1983) and Neal of Newton's *I Will Call It Georgie's Blues* (1983) are talented yet have difficulties adjusting to adolescence. They both feel different from their peers. Yet, they are not social misfits. Both are sensitive individuals who try to help others. Neal is attentive to his younger brother Georgie, who seems so intense and troubled. Carrie shares the beauty of creativity and fantasy with a younger child and develops new, close relationships with family and friends.

I Keep Coming Back to Something Inside Me

Individuals' achievements can start first by following an intuition that starts at the visceral level. They may repeatedly draw or write something in order to sort through information and clarify their thoughts. Eventually, feelings and experiences can crystallize through artistic expression, and a form of self-understanding emerges. This self-knowledge is a compelling source of thinking and action.

In *The Language of Goldfish*, Carrie sees a psychiatrist while recovering from her suicide attempt. As she begins to do her artwork again, she repeatedly draws a picture of the island in the backyard. The doctor wants Carrie to answer her own question about why she draws this island so frequently. Eventually, she can explain why she became ill. Carrie recognizes that she found growing up harder than most. The painting represents her vision of fantasy, imagination, and retreat both before and after her illness.

Other protagonists write in order to sort through their experiences. In Hinton's *The Outsiders* (1967), Ponyboy begins a written summary in order to share the experiences of rival gang members. In Chris Crutcher's *Chinese Handcuffs* (1989), Dillon composes letters to his brother who committed suicide. Lorraine and John of Zindel's *The Pigman* (1968) write their story in order to clarify experiences with an older friend who dies. Whether the artistic product is writing, painting, or music, each protagonist's outpouring crystallizes what was inside his or her head.

Young adult novels illustrate how individuals seek authenticity in their artistic work. Their search resembles Erik Erikson's concept of fidelity. In Gary Paulsen's *Sentries* (1986), one protagonist, Peter, is a musician who plays in a successful band. Despite the band's success, he feels as if something is missing in their work. Peter recalls one night when he and his band began to jam spontaneously with other musicians while they were traveling. The music soared that evening. Knowing how genuine that piece is, Peter now wants to create a new work based on that experience. He writes an inspiring song and brings it to the other artists. They share his enthusiasm. The band practices, improvises, and eventually plays the music at Red Rocks. It has an electric effect on the audience. Everyone detects how original this music is.

In Brooks' *Midnight Hour Encores* (1986), Sib performs beautifully during an audition. She describes how the performance makes her feel inside:

> I've never been hotter . . . this is one of those days when every nuance of technique and intellect and emotion finds its way into the fingertips . . . I am everywhere and everything on the instrument, high and low, quick and slow, slippery and chopped . . . I close my eyes too, and instead of feeling myself play the music I seem too to be a listener, evoking the music by hearing it a millionth of a note before it comes. (254–255)

This flow emerges as people explore and integrate different components of their lives.

Finding Our Milieu: It Fits Just Like a Glove

When we find our own milieu, fluid expression can emerge. This discovery is a central theme in young adult literature. In Hannah Green's *I Never Promised You a Rose Garden* (1964), the protagonist, who recovers from mental illness, begins to see her own gift in art. Deborah always communicates through her art work even when she is very ill in the hospital. Yet, it isn't until she is healthier and recalls with her doctor a dream about a friend that Deborah fully recognizes her talent. This insight feels like a personal awakening to her.

Carrie of Oneal's *The Language of Goldfish* (1983) is able to find her niche, just as her art teacher predicts. Her best drawings begin to emerge, reflecting how much richer her life is. Despite a classmate's ridicule that "Everybody knows you're different," Carrie is more immersed in life and does not retreat from family, peers, or school. She meets a boy in math class who also understands what it feels like to be different. Carrie's friendship with him and others indicates that she has developed important connections to other people instead of withdrawing.

Carrie of *The Language of Goldfish* and Neal of Newton's *I Will Call It Georgie's Blues* (1983) both illustrate the connection between our inner and outer world. For example, when Carrie's life was less enriched, she felt as if her paintings and drawings were "dead." However, as her life becomes more dynamic, her paintings and artwork flourish and display color, as well as richness. Neal gradually recognizes that concealing an important part of himself constricts his relationships with family and peers. Abundant expression emerges for him as he stops hiding his passionate love of music. Finding our niche involves openness rather than closure since it removes stagnation and dullness.

The Intangible Rewards of Success

How we handle success and integrate achievement into our self-concepts is an ongoing process and lifetime achievement. Many will learn to better enjoy their successes. Recently, I heard one local high school athlete on television say, "It means much more because we had to work so hard to achieve this goal." Her insight corrects our common tendency to see a final product or achievement that is extraordinary and believe it came naturally to people. Throughout our lives, the successes we feel are much richer inside when we have to work so hard to attain a goal. That feeling of exhilaration and pride is immeasurable. Countless hours of preparation offer their own rewards as well. How often do we compare ourselves to people who achieve a goal without much toil, forgetting that they rarely tackle anything that is hard for them?

The authors and protagonists of young adult literature illustrate how artistic and scientific achievement entails disciplined effort, training, and self-understanding. Like us, the protagonists can feel impatient about the delay of gratification when the results are not visible for a long time. Whether it is music, writing, or painting, an artistic product represents an outpouring of something intensely personal from an individual's inner world.

Protagonists of young adult literature do not have the easy, glamorous successes of Hollywood stories. Their achievement requires steady exertion. In Davis' *If Rock and Roll Were a Machine* (1992), a teacher named Tanneran encourages Bert to be a writer. Recognizing Bert's talent, Tanneran reminds Bert that to be good at anything requires immense effort and patience. In addition, this instructor tells Bert to ". . . be thankful for the pain in his life, not resentful, because out of that pain would come knowledge" (125).

In Brooks' *Midnight Hour Encores* (1986), Sib, a talented musician, is also reminded of one of the sources for her energy by a friend who asks her, "Where do you think you get your feeling that you can do anything? Your spontaneity, your talent, your freedom from doubt? . . . You deserve what you have, yes. But you have it because of love. Loving someone is the only way you get that kind of energy and daring. That kind of freedom. And you've had that for a long time, Sib" (244).

We can enjoy successes. However, the temporariness of winning or losing also surfaces, as illustrated in young adult fiction. For example, in Crutcher's *Running Loose* (1983), a friend reminds Louie that there are other valuable priorities in life besides being a star football player and that ultimately Louie will have to decide what is most important to him (90).

What We Would Do Differently Next Time

Achievement includes coping adaptively with defeat. The ability to deal constructively with disappointments and to learn from mistakes is linked to Robert Sternberg's views of intelligence and to the development of emotional autonomy (Atwater 1992, 140). The ability to rebound from setbacks and defeat is devalued by our society, but it is a valuable inner resource. In literature and life, this skill can set examples to others, spearhead change, and reduce the fear of taking risks. Several protagonists of young adult literature voice their concern about making a mistake as they train for competition. Their teachers and friends advise them not to let fear of committing errors keep them from doing challenging work.

Lois Duncan's *Daughters of Eve* (1979) illustrates how young people use failure as a learning experience. In this novel, a young man named Gordon feels sorry that fellow student Fran Schneider is eliminated from the state science competition. Fran acknowledges to Gordon that she is disappointed but recognizes why she was disqualified from the competition: She kept her science project a secret from her teacher. Her project involved animals and she was unaware that there were specific guidelines for conducting such research. Gordon, who was selected for the competition, admits that he probably did mediocre work because he did not think there would be any contest at all. He acknowledges now that he knows better. Gordon and Fran are open with each other about their projects, and their talk about setbacks and defeat is the basis for a new friendship.

Conclusion

Teachers meet people with a wide range of talents who underestimate themselves, imitate originality, or do not work to the best of their ability and effort. Dwelling on our academic abilities alone misses important sources of achievement. Society's focus on visible signs of success and our tendency to devalue effort sidetrack us from realizing the rich potential inside us. Adolescence is a time of valuable exploration. Finding our own milieus and discovering the intangible rewards of effort and discipline are based on self-understanding and hard work. As young adult literature and psychological studies illustrate, this effort produces fluid expression in both our inner and outer worlds.

Works Cited

Armstrong, T. 1994. *Multiple Intelligences in the Classroom.* Alexandria, VA: Association for Supervision and Curriculum Development.

Atwater, E. 1992. *Adolescence.* 3d. ed. Englewood Cliffs, NJ: Prentice-Hall.

Avi. 1990. *The True Confessions of Charlotte Doyle.* New York: Avon.

———. 1991. *Nothing But the Truth.* New York: Avon.

Brooks, B. 1986. *Midnight Hour Encores.* New York: HarperKeypoint.

Carter, A. R. 1989. *Up Country.* New York: Scholastic.

Cobb, N. J. 1995. *Adolescence: Continuity, Change and Diversity.* 2d ed. Mountain View, CA: Mayfield.

Crew, L. 1989. *Children of the River.* New York: Dell.

Crutcher, C. 1983. *Running Loose.* New York: Dell.

———. 1989. *Chinese Handcuffs.* New York: Dell.

Dacey, J., and M. Kenny. 1994. *Adolescent Development.* Madison, WI: WCB Brown & Benchmark.

Davis, T. 1992. *If Rock and Roll Were a Machine.* New York: Bantam Doubleday Dell Books.

Duncan, L. 1979. *Daughters of Eve.* New York: Dell.

Eccles, J., C. Midgley, A. Wigfield, C. M. Buchanan, D. Reuman, C. Flanagan, and D. Mac Iver. 1993. "Development During Adolescence: The Impact of Stage-Environment Fit on Young Adolescents' Experiences in Schools and in Families." *American Psychologist* 48(2): 90–101.

Fuhrmann, B. S. 1990. *Adolescence, Adolescents.* 2d ed. Glenview, IL: Scott, Foresman and Company.

Green, H. 1964. *I Never Promised You a Rose Garden.* New York: New American Library.

Hinton, S. 1967. *The Outsiders.* New York: Dell.

Lowry, L. 1977. *A Summer to Die.* New York: Bantam Doubleday Dell.

Melby, J. N., and R. Conger. 1996. "Parental Behaviors and Adolescent Academic Performance: A Longitudinal Analysis." *Journal of Research on Adolescence* 6(1): 113–137.

Newton, S. 1983. *I Will Call It Georgie's Blues.* New York: Puffin Books.

Oneal, Z. 1983. *The Language of Goldfish.* New York: Puffin.

Paterson, K. 1978. *The Great Gilly Hopkins.* New York: HarperCollins.

Paulsen, G. 1986. *Sentries.* New York: Puffin.

———. 1993. *Sisters.* San Diego: Harcourt Brace & Company.

Pipher, M. 1994. *Reviving Ophelia: Saving the Selves of Adolescent Girls.* New York: Ballantine Books.

Reaver, C. 1992. *A Little Bit Dead.* New York: Bantam Doubleday Dell Books.

Steinberg, L. 1993. *Adolescence.* 3d. ed. New York: McGraw-Hill.

Steinberg, L., and A. Levine. 1990. *You and Your Adolescent: A Parent's Guide for Ages Ten to Twenty.* New York: Harper & Row.

Sternberg, R. J. 1995. "For Whom the Bell Curve Tolls: A Review of the Bell Curve." *Psychological Science* 6(5): 257–261.

Voigt, C. 1981. *Homecoming*. New York: Ballantine Books.

———. 1982. *Dicey's Song*. New York: Ballantine Books.

Zindel, P. 1968. *The Pigman*. Toronto: Bantam Books.

Six

Right from Wrong
I Wish I Knew What to Do

There is no codebook available today to tell us correct answers to predicaments. The world is full of contradictory messages, and we are faced with dilemmas throughout our lives. Many people in our society experience affronts to human dignity and contend with disillusionment and loss of hope. Each person's individuality can be tested in subtle and overt ways by peer groups or authority. Moral choices are not easy. How can we make brave and thoughtful decisions? Teachers play an instrumental role in helping their students counteract disillusionment, question injustice, and make realistic appraisals of authority. By promoting an ethic of care and compassion in our classrooms, we can help students to develop faith in their own voices and to develop moral courage.

What Do I Do Now? The Moral Dilemmas in Young Adult Literature

I Want Everyone to Like Me

Mirroring life, young adult literature illustrates how teenagers struggle to win the approval of their family, other authority figures, or their peer group. Many of us strive for social acceptance. Both men and women feel pressure to behave according to people's expectations. The struggle between remaining connected to others and remaining true to ourselves is intricately tied to the lifelong process of identity development and the attainment of emotional autonomy.

This concern also reflects tensions in moral development. Lawrence Kohlberg and others document that adolescents and adults in the United States often reason at the Conventional level of moral development, which emphasizes conformity to the group and obedience to authority. At this level, individuals initially focus upon winning the approval of people they are close to, such as family, other adults, teachers (in the elementary school years), or the peer group (in the junior high school years) (Sprinthall and Collins 1995, 211–217). Later, people at the Conventional level can shift their loyalties to a larger group and obey laws in order to protect the community's welfare. These individuals recognize the value of laws and do not view societal regulations as transitory or arbitrary. However, they have difficulty resolving conflicts between laws and are uncomfortable challenging authority (Santrock 1996, 422–425). High school students and others who utilize Conventional thinking can be unbending and narrow in their interpretation of regulations (Steinberg and Levine 1990, 295–296).

Conventional moral reasoning is illustrated in Elisabeth Speare's *The Witch of Blackbird Pond* (1958). In this novel, there are adults in the Puritan community who are inflexible about obeying the law. Their dogmatic views result in stereotypical thinking and conformity. In general, these people are suspicious of individuals who defy convention. However, their thinking is also partially based on a desire to guard the town's general welfare.

Blind Faith

Young adult literature illustrates how individuals might begin allegiance to a larger community by obeying all forms of authority. Some people may not move past this blind faith. Others can eventually realize the cost for such obedience and are tormented by their actions. For example, in Robert Cormier's *After the First Death* (1989), a father's loyalty and duty to his country go too far. The father, General Marchand, works with other officials in order to save the lives of children who have been captured by terrorists. The hijackers threaten the security of a top secret project called Inner Delta, which is important for the country's security. Eventually, the General sacrifices his own son, Ben, as a messenger to the terrorists. One of the puzzles in this novel is how Ben dies. The father is never the same after his son's death. Haunting scenes in this novel suggest that the General becomes insane after realizing how he betrayed Ben.

Other young adult novels show how people discover that they have been exploited when they thought they were honoring their family, their peers, their country, or the work ethic. In Gary Paulsen's *Sentries* (1986), young men serve their country in the military for wars that are brutal and senseless. Paulsen vividly describes how several soldiers are mentally and physically destroyed by combat. One soldier, caught in the war machine, hesitates to kill a child while fighting. His fellow soldiers tell him he must shoot in order to protect others. He fires at this child, but the violence incapacitates him. Overall, the vignettes in *Sentries* reveal how fragile human dignity and personal awakening are when there is perpetual trauma in our society.

I Cannot Do This

A crisis can occur when people's beliefs oppose other individuals or a group. They may fear reprisal when they voice opposition. However, moral conflicts can also stimulate people to form clearer ideas about who they are and what their most important values are, even if those values go against a group. After experimenting with different roles and values, individuals who develop a distinct identity become less concerned about trying to please everyone. Having strength in their own convictions enables young adults and others to withstand disapproval.

When individuals stand up for their own convictions, they can be taunted or victimized by a peer group or gang. The taunting can test their ability to remain true to themselves. There is no cheering crowd to remind them of how brave they are. In fact, just the opposite reaction can occur. In Robert Cormier's *The Chocolate War* (1974), Jerry Renault asks, "Do I dare disturb the universe?" (142). He wonders whether it is worth it to upset the status quo at his school because anyone who does is hated, ostracized, and attacked. There is both a physical and emotional toll for Jerry. Ironically, a nonconformist such as Jerry can experience more anguish than people who commit crimes or conform.

In Bette Greene's *The Drowning of Stephan Jones* (1991), Carla is willing to do anything in order to be accepted into the peer group and be Andy Harris' girlfriend. However, there is a cost for her popularity. Carla does not forcefully protest or argue with her boyfriend about his heinous actions until violence erupts. Then she faces a moral conflict. When Andy and his peer group viciously attack a homosexual, who dies, she can no longer remain silent. Carla stands up for her beliefs and testifies in court against Andy and his peers.

A related theme centers on how young people are torn between loyalty to the larger group at school or the community and their desire to protect the rights and freedom of the individual. In novels such as *The Chocolate War* (1974), Lois Duncan's *Daughters of Eve* (1979), and Chris Crutcher's *Running Loose* (1983), adolescents are drawn to a group such as a football team, a clique, or a gang at school that terrorizes, dominates, or excludes others. When the group begins to intimidate others, some participants experience conflicts because they know that what the group is doing is wrong. Yet, in each story, authentic nonconformists begin a lonely trek of disobedience when they recognize the dangers of losing their autonomy.

The fight to preserve one's individuality is also illustrated in Lois Lowry's novel *The Giver* (1993). The story describes what happens when people sacrifice their identity to a community that has erased human emotions and richness from life. One elderly man, who is called "The Giver," is the only person who stores memories. He feels all the pain and emotions for the entire community. The protagonist, twelve-year-old Jonas, is selected to be the next "receiver" of memory. He begins as an apprentice with the elderly man in order to learn how he will fulfill his new role. However, Jonas slowly discovers the horror of this colorless society and decides to escape. His departure protects his individuality and gives him the opportunity to feel human.

Now I Know Better

The work of Mary Belenky and colleagues illuminates how women who place too much trust in men's expertise or power may face a turning point (Belenky et al. 1986, 57–58). Some individuals can develop more faith in their own intuition and skill as they recognize sources of silence, submission, and empowerment. Realistic changes in adolescents' views of authority can lead to positive growth, even after they discover they were naive and that others had deceived them. Courage can grow from this loss of idealism. These qualities enable people to surprise others by unexpectedly defying the status quo, standing up for their own beliefs, or rebelling.

Young adult literature examines how adolescents as well as adults begin a journey of self-discovery once they recognize the cost of their blind obedience and naive respect for powerful people. In Avi's *The True Confessions of Charlotte Doyle* (1990), the protagonist, Charlotte, travels on a ship with a captain and his crew. During her difficult voyage, Charlotte redefines her concepts of authority. This young woman's absolute faith in the captain's integrity shatters when she discovers his abuse of the crew. She reevaluates her commitment to fairness, discovers fortitude, preserves her own dignity, and wins the crew's admiration through discipline. She endures humiliation and setbacks and learns to trust her own sound judgment.

Where Is My Rainbow?

How often do individuals in literature and life look for a rainbow at the end of a long, difficult journey only to discover instead that what-ever they had saved up for has evaporated despite their hard work and honesty? They may have focused on a wish as a survival technique. Their subsequent disillusionment dissipates with a change in perspective. Although they do not see a tangible reward after much mental and physical endurance, some protagonists rediscover hope and new direction in their lives.

In Linda Crew's *Children of the River* (1989), Sundara uses a dream in order to endure silence. She feels divided by conflicting values. Sundara wants to fit into the American culture but also feels pressure from her family to accept traditional customs. Initially, in order to resolve her dilemma, she severs the relationship with her American boyfriend, Jonathan. This sacrifice is tolerable as long as she can dream about being reunited with her boyfriend in Cambodia. Sundara is devastated when she discovers that this young man has died. After a period of withdrawal and grieving, Sundara opens up to her aunt and expresses feelings that had been buried for years. She discloses her own guilt about a baby dying in her care as they traveled from Cambodia to the United States. Lifting the burden enables her to find a new sense of purpose and meaning in her life.

Missing How Brave We Really Are

Adolescents and adults can overlook how brave they are because they compare themselves to others or search for visible signs of boldness. It is also possible, as Bette Greene observes, that our culture often focuses too much on physical courage and devalues moral courage (Alvine 1994, 5–9). Notice how frequently men are encouraged to demonstrate physical prowess as a sign of vigor.

Teachers and psychologists tell me how frequently young adults remain unaware of their own boldness as they resist peer pressure, admit errors, or seek help. Genuine courage is hard to detect because those who speak loudest, act daringly, or behave with bravado may lack sustaining courage. Their audacious acts may be a form of superficial denial of their fears. The realization that bravery is subjective offers a realistic antidote. One person can do something easily and it does not require bravery because they are not afraid. Another individual who tries to conquer fear is daring.

In Robert Cormier's *After the First Death* (1989), the female protagonist, Kate, develops much courage as she struggles to save the lives of children who are hostages of terrorists. Kate has always thought of herself as fearful and nervous. She is constantly embarrassed by having problems controlling her bladder. Using every resource she has, Kate attempts to outsmart the terrorists and keep the children calm. As readers, we want her to grasp what a heroine she is. When she is killed, her death becomes even more tragic because she will not have the opportunity to develop an internal conviction about her own bravery. People who demonstrate high moral standards are valuable role models, but we cannot wait for outside confirmation as a reward or incentive for developing these principles ourselves.

Am I Telling the Whole Truth or Am I Deceiving Others?

As the books of Harriet Lerner (1989, 1993) and other psychologists illuminate, establishing healthy boundaries offers safety and freedom. Boundaries should be both permeable and impermeable. They also enable people to preserve their individuality and maintain close connections in valuable relationships. In contrast, constant false fronts become barriers to intimacy and personal growth.

In Virginia Wolff's *Make Lemonade* (1993), fourteen-year-old LaVaughn attends "Steam Class," which is designed to improve teens' self-esteem and coping skills. During this class, she describes her search for safe, healthy boundaries when she says:

> . . . Boundaries,
> and how you keep hold of them for safety
> not to let them get out of control.
> If you got hurt too bad when you were little
> you don't know your boundaries good,
> you could let people in too close & they hurt you
> or you keep them way far away & they can't help you
> and Steam Class is where you help figure it out. (103)

There is a similar struggle negotiating the boundaries of truth and deception for the protagonist of Alice Childress' *Rainbow Jordan* (1981). Rainbow, who is fourteen years old, learns about the kinds of small lies that are protective. For example, she and her adult friend Josephine decide it's fine to lie a little about your age, to use lipstick, and wear cosmetics. But, as they both discover, it's important to stay away from the big lies. Rainbow finally acknowledges the realistic truth about why her mom is in and out of her life, and Josephine is more honest about why her husband left her. Both are then able to make positive steps toward change, and they become closer.

Several young adult novels describe how adolescents negotiate the boundaries between truth and deception. Both literature and life illustrate how much truth is based on our own viewing angle and definition of reality (see Chapter 4). We recognize a gray area; what might be right for one person may not be right for another, and there are degrees of candor and falseness.

Bruce Brooks' *The Moves Make the Man* (1984) highlights the complexity of truth and deception by describing how two adolescents negotiate honesty in relationships. Bix Rivers plays basketball strictly by the rules and resists learning the fake moves from his friend Jerome. As

Jerome explains, however, such maneuvers are legitimate ways to improve your game and handle competition so that you are not so obvious to all rivals. Eventually, Bix is willing to learn how to perform the fakeouts on the court in order to win a confrontational basketball game against his stepfather. Here, his movements make him better at competition. Later, however, he pulls the ultimate fakeout when he and Jerome visit his mother at a hospital. Faced with the truth that his own mom, who is emotionally ill, no longer recognizes him, he turns away and pretends that a patient in another bed is his mother. This quick move saves face, but Bix immediately disappears from town. His departure from friends and family prevents the realization of truth that could enhance personal growth.

Young adult fiction vividly portrays how on the surface it looks as if slick, smooth operators win, but how they really don't. In Avi's *Nothing But the Truth* (1990), Philip Malloy defies a teacher who gave him a low grade. He acts and speaks as if he were telling nothing but the truth. His real incentive, however, is petty. One lie snowballs in the political system of a school. Philip's defiance is distorted by the media, and he is labeled a champion of freedom. It is impossible for this young man to admit his actual motivation as the distortion grows. He is famous by media reports but unhappy inside. Eventually, Philip stops attending classes because he thinks the other kids hate him and he transfers to another school. The deception has a big impact on him. At the conclusion of the novel, Philip's internal demons are a chilling reminder of what he lost.

Our Internal Moral Victories

Discovering the value of internal moral victories enables people to withstand physical defeat and develop moral courage, even if it appears to the outside world that they failed. An internal moral victory occurs for Carla, the female protagonist in *The Drowning of Stephan Jones* (Greene 1991). It is initially hard for Carla to see her triumph because she loses her friends. However, she wins in the long term by having the courage to testify about injustice.

In Robert Cormier's *Tunes for Bears to Dance To* (1992), the protagonist, Henry, also experiences an internal moral achievement. After settling into a new community with his family, he becomes friends with Mr. Levine, who has survived the Holocaust. As their friendship develops, Mr. Levine shows Henry his special carved reproduction of a small town. When Mr. Hairston, Henry's employer, asks Henry to secretly smash Mr. Levine's beautiful village, Henry is torn. Mr. Hairston takes advantage of Henry's innocent desire to do well for his family by telling him,

And think about this: If I can't trust you to do this little thing for me, how can I trust you anymore here in the store?. . . . Know what else, Henry? I will have to spread the word about you to other merchants. That you are not to be trusted. No one will ever hire you again. (72)

Henry does smash the village, but only by accident. Just as Henry decides *not* to lower a mallet to destroy the village, he is surprised by the movement of a rat. The mallet falls and the village is smashed. As Henry recognizes later, the important victory for him is that he ultimately defeats Mr. Hairston by not completing the bargain. He refuses to accept the grocer's payback. Despite his loss of innocence, Henry has preserved his integrity.

Am I Being Selfish?

Themes in Carol Gilligan's research on moral development and female adolescents' development are also prominent in young adult fiction. In her book *In a Different Voice* (1982), Gilligan describes differences in men's and women's reasoning about morality. Women focus on compassion and care in their moral choices, whereas men center on rights and justice. Gilligan proposes that these differences are not black-and-white. Men and women can express both perspectives, and the most advanced morality blends compassion with objective focus on rights and justice. Also, higher levels of moral reasoning integrate concern for self with concern for others rather than dwelling exclusively on self or sacrifice for others (Rice 1996, 315–316).

A good example of women's struggle to integrate concern for others with concern for self is illustrated in Speare's *The Witch of Blackbird Pond* (1958). The protagonist, Kit, loses hope and spirit when she is reprimanded for her unconventional ways in this strict community. She is a caring, sensitive individual. As her cousins develop a serious fever, Kit works hard to complete neglected chores, make meals, and care for the sick. Her devotion to others is admirable. She also struggles to balance this compassion with concern for her own well-being. Kit gradually realizes that excessive silence and submission is stifling. An elderly woman, Hannah, befriends Kit, and helps her to recognize the importance of listening to her own voice. Eventually, Kit saves Hannah's life with great courage. Kit also wins the admiration of her relatives, who begin to soften their rigid, authoritarian interpretation of the law when they recognize how atrocious the community's witch hunt is. Her aunt and uncle increasingly appreciate all that Kit does for other people. Kit demonstrates concern for a little girl's education, protects Hannah, and respects her relatives' values. In addition, she remains true to herself.

Sue Ellen Bridgers' *Notes for Another Life* (1981) also illustrates a young woman's struggle to balance the ethic of care for others with responsibility toward one's own well-being. In this novel, Wren Jackson and her brother Kevin deal with many changes and losses in their family. Their mother has left home to pursue her career, and their father, who is mentally ill, resides in a hospital. Both learn the value of reaching out to others, and they gradually develop a stronger sense of their own identities. Wren describes a new realization to her brother Kevin:

> There are so many things I have to decide for myself, Kevin. It's like there are spaces inside, separate places for music and for Sam, for you and our family, for school. But there's another place just for me. Right now I feel as if I have to take special care of that place that's just mine because it's where I can be honest with myself and decide what's right for me no matter what other people want. Is that selfish? (192)

In my classes, I have heard both men and women voice similar concerns as they juggle complex commitments.

Conclusion

Interpretations of our outer world can create disillusionment, blind faith, or idealism. However, adolescents and adults can find positive value in honoring the values of family, peers, and society. Advancements in moral development occur when people develop internal standards of right and wrong and recognize the gray areas of morality. Achieving internal moral victories, negotiating boundaries, and discovering that courage is subjective are examples of positive outcomes from moral crises. The development of moral strength hinges on viewing both our inner world and outer world in less black-and-white terms.

Works Cited

Alvine, L. 1994. "Understanding Adolescent Homophobia: An Interview with Bette Greene." *The Alan Review* 21(2): 5–9.

Avi. 1990. *The True Confessions of Charlotte Doyle*. New York: Avon.

————. 1991. *Nothing But the Truth*. New York: Avon.

Belenky, M. F., B. M. Clinchy, N. R. Goldberger, and J. M. Tarule. 1986. *Women's Ways of Knowing: The Development of Self, Voice, and Mind*. New York: Basic Books.

Bridgers, S. E. 1981. *Notes for Another Life*. New York: Bantam Books.

Brooks, B. 1984. *The Moves Make the Man.* New York: HarperKeypoint.

Childress, A. 1981. *Rainbow Jordan.* New York: Avon Books.

Cormier, R. 1974. *The Chocolate War.* New York: Dell.

———. 1989. *After the First Death.* New York: Dell.

———. 1992. *Tunes for Bears to Dance To.* New York: Dell.

Crew, L. 1989. *Children of the River.* New York: Dell.

Crutcher, C. 1983. *Running Loose.* New York: Dell.

Duncan, L. 1979. *Daughters of Eve.* New York: Dell.

Gilligan, C. 1982. *In a Different Voice: Psychological Theory and Women's Development.* Cambridge, MA: Harvard University Press.

Greene, B. 1991. *The Drowning of Stephan Jones.* New York: Bantam Books.

Lerner, H. 1989. *The Dance of Intimacy: A Women's Guide to Courageous Acts of Change.* New York: Harper & Row.

———. 1993. *The Dance of Deception: Pretending and Truth-Telling in Women's Lives.* New York: HarperCollins.

Lowry, L. 1993. *The Giver.* New York: Dell.

Paulsen, G. 1986. *Sentries.* New York: Puffin.

Rice, F. P. 1996. *The Adolescent: Development, Relationships, and Culture.* 8th ed. Boston: Allyn & Bacon.

Santrock, J. W. 1996. *Adolescence: An Introduction.* 6th ed. Madison, WI: Brown & Benchmark.

Speare, E. G. 1958. *The Witch of Blackbird Pond.* New York: Dell.

Sprinthall, N. A., and W. A. Collins. 1995. *Adolescent Psychology: A Developmental View.* 3d ed. New York: McGraw-Hill.

Steinberg, L., and A. Levine. 1990. *You and Your Adolescent: A Parent's Guide for Ages Ten to Twenty.* New York: Harper & Row.

Wolff, V. E. 1993. *Make Lemonade.* New York: Scholastic.

Seven

My Sexuality
Fantasy Versus Reality

Sexuality influences every aspect of our lives, including family functioning, peer relationships, morality, and physical development. Adolescence brings significant changes in teenagers' sexual relationships. Through education, experience, and insight, young adults can develop realistic, positive views of sexuality instead of relying on extremely romantic or negative images. Nonetheless, clarifying the role of fantasy and reality in sexual development is difficult in our culture because there are such contradictory messages from parents, schools, church, peers, and the media.

Exploring topics such as sexuality, cultural messages of beauty, and romantic relationships in young adult literature and adolescent psychology can benefit teachers and students. Comparing realistic and unrealistic standards of intimacy by examining the emotional and psychological aspects of sexual development is valuable at any age. Experts in adolescent psychology describe the type of information that would be beneficial for teenagers:

> What adolescents need is much better information about their bodies, the bodies of the other sex, the psychology of human relationships, a chance to explore and question their own attitudes and beliefs, and above all some help in learning how to communicate intimately, i.e., how to talk about feelings, sex, contraception, fidelity, and trust to name just a few important topics. (Kimmel and Weiner 1995, citing Sarrel and Sarrel, 348)

Affirming a healthy sexual identity is an important developmental task of adolescence. Contrary to popular stereotypes, however, teenagers in the 1990s are not a sex-crazed generation (Steinberg and Levine 1990, 236), nor do the majority of adolescents condone extreme sexual permissiveness in the absence of caring relationships. Teenagers' priorities will shift:

> In early adolescence, youngsters are concerned about who they are sexually, where these new sensations and feelings are coming from, and what to think about sex. In middle adolescence, young people worry about what they personally should do about sex, about what role sex should play in their lives. (Steinberg and Levine 1990, 238)

Adolescents' initial interpretations of these new feelings and changes are illustrated in many young adult novels. In Robert Cormier's *Fade* (1988), thirteen-year-old Paul is mesmerized by his aunt. Internally, he is

> wondering what was happening to [him], happy and sad, hot and cold, all at the same time, [his] heart filled to bursting with—what?—what? [He] couldn't put a name to it. (11)

Feelings of exhilaration are reflected in novels such as Judy Blume's *Forever* (1975), Maureen Daly's *Seventeenth Summer* (1942), and Anne Frank's *The Diary of a Young Girl* (1995). During her adolescence, Anne writes about her sexuality in positive ways: "I think that what's happening to me is so wonderful, and I don't just mean the changes taking place on the outside of my body, but also those on the inside" (161).

Adolescents need time to sort through their feelings, and they benefit from parents' reassurances that their experiences are normal. It is not uncommon for mothers and fathers to feel uncomfortable discussing sex with their sons and daughters (Kimmel and Weiner 1995, 347). However, some parents aim for better communication. Teenagers gain from open dialogues about sexuality, and they often want to obtain more information from their parents.

Mixed Emotions

Since sexuality influences many aspects of our lives, it stirs complicated, mixed emotions. Young people can experience diverse and extreme feelings of curiosity, freedom, maturity, fear, and guilt. Mental-health professionals sometimes describe adolescence as a semiperpetual borderline state. This borderline state includes "splitting," which refers partially to adolescents' black-and-white thinking and to the tendency to split the bad from the good. As a result, once adolescents see flaws in a person, they may temporarily perceive the person as all bad, losing touch with the previous good aspects of the same individual. Many of us think this way, but we vary in terms of how much or how often we rely upon such reasoning. Teenagers display more extreme versions of this dynamic.

Adolescents' initial black-and-white thinking regarding sexuality surfaces in novels such as Bette Greene's *The Drowning of Stephan Jones* (1991). At first, the female protagonist, Carla, describes her concepts of masculinity and femininity in black-and-white terms when she feels puzzled about cultural standards. She thinks, "Male? Female? Don't you have to be one thing or the other? If you're not one thing then don't you definitely have to be the other? At this point, the only thing that [Carla] was convinced of was her own confusion" (14–15).

Another example of splitting occurs in Daly's *Seventeenth Summer* (1942). In this story, the protagonist, Angie Morrow, invites her boyfriend, Jack Duluth, to dinner with her family one night. The dinner does not go well. Jack is awkward and fumbles in his table manners. She suddenly sees him in a new light and is struck by how her upbringing differs from his less-polished background. How could he tap his spoon against his teeth while eating ice cream at her home in front of her family? During the evening, she thinks,

> It all seemed so suddenly and sickenly clear—I could just see his father in shirt sleeves, folding food onto his knife and never using napkins except when there was company. And probably they brought the coffee pot right in and set it on the table. My whole mind was filled with a growing disdain and loathing. His family probably didn't even own a butter knife! No girl has to stand all that. Never. (168)

Her response is temporary however. Later, she regrets how cold she was toward Jack that evening.

Adolescents' semiperpetual borderline state also includes ambivalence toward the social world. They can seek sexual encounters but flee them as well. Young adult novels such as Cormier's *Fade* (1988) illustrate this pattern of approach and withdrawal. The protagonist, Paul, is enthralled and repelled by his sexual attraction to his aunt. There are repeated images of Paul pursuing and fleeing sexual experiences. He feels elation, joy, and curiosity about his sexuality. Yet, guilt often swallows him. For example, during a church confession, Paul debates exactly what to say to a priest about his forbidden acts. As he leaves the confessional, he asks himself, "Would the sinning never stop?" (92).

In Katherine Paterson's *Jacob Have I Loved* (1980), Louise is shaken by her mixed sexual feelings toward the older man whom she and her friend Call have nicknamed "the Captain":

> I had not put my arms around another person since I was tiny. It may have been the unaccustomed closeness, I don't know. I had only meant to comfort him, but as I smelled his sweat and felt the spring of his beard against my cheek, an alarm began to clang inside my body. I went hot all over, and I could hear my heart banging to

be let out of my chest. "Let go, stupid," part of me was saying, while another voice I hardly recognized was urging me to hold him tighter. (132)

The ambivalence decreases as young people become more clear about their sexual identities.

Sexuality and Family Relationships

Recent psychological studies reveal increased tension in the home as teenage sons and daughters experience significant changes during puberty. Adolescents' physical development influences social relationships and vice versa (Steinberg 1993, 139; Sprinthall and Collins 1995, 256). As John Dacey and Maureen Kenny describe in their text *Adolescent Development* (1994), parents and other adults respond with different expectancies to teenagers' changing physical appearance, and this shift affects family interactions (218, citing Peterson). The connection between pubertal changes and increased family disagreements is illustrated in Hadley Irwin's *Abby, My Love* (1985). The protagonist, Chip, describes the new conflicts with his mother:

> We always kidded back and forth, Mom and I, but this was different. For some reason, I wanted to say things that would hurt her, but I couldn't tell her that because I didn't know why I felt that way. I'd thought about it a lot. It was sort of an ugly, mean feeling, down deep, so that I felt good after I'd really lashed out at somebody. Not felt good, really. Felt satisfied. Then there was another thing. I didn't like the way I looked. My arms were too long, my legs too short, my head too little, my shoulders too broad. I was sure I looked like a half-grown ape. (25–26)

After puberty, parent-adolescent relationships usually become less tense.

Sexuality and Identity

In his eight-stage model of identity development, Erik Erikson (1968) proposes that individuals need to establish their own identity before they are capable of intimacy. Erikson explains:

> As the young individual seeks at least tentative forms of playful intimacy in friendship and competition, in sex play and love, in argument and gossip, he is apt to experience a peculiar strain, as if such tentative engagement might turn into an interpersonal fusion amounting to a loss of identity and requiring, therefore, a tense inner reservation, a caution in commitment. (167)

Carol Gilligan, Harriet Lerner, Ruthellen Josselson, and others describe intricate connections among identity, intimacy, and conflict based on more recent research and clinical work with men and women (see Chapter 1). There are examples in young adult fiction of protagonists who work to establish a clearer identity before they develop healthy bonds with their boyfriends or girlfriends. Without a firm sense of identity, some cling to others for happiness, or wonder, "If I become close, will I still be my own person?"

Several protagonists in young adult fiction voice this concern. For example, in Sue Ellen Bridgers' *Notes for Another Life* (1987), the protagonist, Wren, cares about her boyfriend, Sam. As they become closer, Wren realizes how important it will be to develop her own identity and nurture her relationships with Sam, her family, and peers. She becomes aware that her interest in music is more important to her than she initially realized. Sam respects Wren's goals and admits that he had not been aware of how she felt.

Wren's brother, Kevin, and his girlfriend, Melanie, struggle with a similar issue. Kevin deals with his anger, guilt, and grief over significant losses in his own life. As he recovers from an attempted suicide, he learns how important it is to develop his own identity. He also stops blaming others. Gradually, Kevin becomes less distant and more caring in his relationships. He refrains from using his relationship with Melanie to avoid confronting his conflicts.

Other protagonists also recognize that they cannot use relationships as a crutch for solving their own problems. In Sue Ellen Bridgers' *Permanent Connections* (1987), the protagonist, Rob, develops an important relationship with a young woman named Ellery. Over time, however, Ellery feels that the relationship is too intense. Rob lashes out at others, takes serious risks, and partially depends on Ellery to escape his troubles. Eventually, Rob's negativity and anger catch up with him. He recognizes how his own unhappiness and irresponsible behaviors affect every aspect of his life. Without detaching from his family, Rob develops the courage to address his own difficulties.

Sexuality and Peers

Adolescents show diverse responses to peer pressure about sexual activity. The authors of an excellent parents' guide on adolescence note:

> Sex has become a status symbol for teenagers. Other symbols of maturity (supporting oneself, living independently, marrying) have been postponed, leaving sex as one of the only available rites of passage to adulthood: If you have had intercourse, you are an adult; if

you are still a virgin, you are just a child. Some teenagers see virgin-
ity as a "ball and chain of innocence" they want to cast off as quickly
as possible. (Steinberg and Levine 1990, 237)

In Daly's *Seventeenth Summer* (1942), Lorraine, who is Angie's
older sister, tries to reassure herself that her own sexual conduct is
normal since standards have become more casual. She tells Angie:

Things are different now from the way they used to be. . . . People
don't think anything of it anymore . . . I mean, if it's only one boy
you're going with and that sort of thing. It isn't like it used to be
when you had to be almost engaged . . . now everybody does it and
nobody thinks . . . you know what I mean. . . . (117)

Angie notices the questioning tone in her sister's voice. Lorraine's
boyfriend, Martin, is using her, yet Lorraine is unwilling to perceive
or fight that injustice. Ultimately, she is hurt by Martin, who drops
her. Although she is more experienced, Lorraine seems discontent
and lonely compared to Angie. Angie's involvement with her boyfriend, Jack, develops more slowly, is less secretive, and is based on
mutual respect. Angie is unsophisticated regarding sexual relationships, but she grows close to Jack, who treats her differently than
other young women whom he has dated.

In Alice Childress' *Rainbow Jordan* (1981), the protagonist, Rainbow, feels constant pressure to have sex with her boyfriend, Eljay. He
keeps reminding her that sex is healthy and that she is too inhibited
and fearful. When Rainbow decides to have sex with Eljay, she is
excited and nervous at the same time. She invites him to her mother's apartment. Eljay arrives with another girlfriend, Janine. Rainbow
finally sees Eljay more accurately and ends the relationship. Her self-
respect grows and she becomes less worried about peer approval.

Other protagonists, such as Louie Banks and Becky in Chris
Crutcher's *Running Loose* (1983), develop intimacy on the basis of
respect rather than because of intimidation or pressure. Although
Louie and Becky share a close, strong relationship, Louie knows he is
not ready to have sex with Becky. She does not pressure Louie about
his decision. Instead, she says:

Sex is scary business, and it's probably best to wait until you're really
ready. I've done it because I thought I was supposed to, and I've
done it because I really wanted to, and let me tell you, supposed to
doesn't cut it. (117–118)

Their relationship reminds us of the important link between positive
self-esteem and responsible sexual decision making.

Sexuality and Morality

The connection between sexuality and morality surfaces in ongoing decisions about equality and reciprocity in relationships. Adolescents and adults who become aware of the underbelly of society can be disillusioned. In several young adult novels such as Lynne Banks' *Melusine: A Mystery* (1988), Hadley Irwin's *Abby, My Love* (1985), Robert Cormier's *Fade* (1988), and Chris Crutcher's *Chinese Handcuffs* (1989), adolescents experience anger, fear, or guilt after they discover something shocking, hidden, or forbidden. Becoming aware of rape, prostitution, and incest deepens the loss of innocence and sense of injustice. Teens as well as adults can recognize how they or other people have been taken advantage of sexually. Victims of sexual exploitation and those exposed to it can experience feelings of trauma, horror, fear, and repulsion. Exposure can also numb or desensitize people so that nothing shocks them anymore.

Fade illustrates adolescents' discovery of this underbelly of society. Because of Paul's special ability to become invisible, he witnesses incest between a brother and sister, observes sex between a shopkeeper and a young adolescent girl, and uncovers other taboo acts. These scenes and his own sexual inclinations stun him. An invisible spy, Paul flees, yet he also returns to see other illicit acts. There is debate in his own head and in some relative's minds about whether his view of reality is accurate or a fantasy.

In *Chinese Handcuffs*, Dillon, the protagonist, sorts through complex feelings about his brother Preston's suicide. Before he commits suicide, Preston tells Dillon about witnessing and participating in the gang rape of a girl at a bar. The scene haunts both brothers. In other novels, such as *Abby, My Love*, men cope with shock and outrage when their girlfriends disclose that they have been sexually abused. The ongoing challenge for these protagonists and people of all ages is to integrate new awareness of the dark side of human nature with a healthy perspective about sexuality rather than to split the bad from the good.

The Cultural Backdrop

Our culture offers many contradictory messages about sexuality, making it harder to integrate its different components. On the one hand, parents, church, or schools urge caution, abstinence, restraint, or asexuality. Yet, the media flaunts sexuality. Magazines, television, music, and movies also promote unrealistic images of romance and physical attractiveness. Psychologist Mary Pipher (1994) notes:

America doesn't have clearly defined and universally accepted rules about sexuality. We live in a pluralistic culture with contradictory sexual paradigms. We hear diverse messages from our families, our churches, our schools and the media, and each of us must integrate these messages and arrive at some value system that makes sense to us. (205)

Evaluating input from parents, peers, schools, church, and the media is an ongoing process for adolescents.

In Linda Crew's *Children of the River* (1989), the protagonist, Sundara, faces contradictory messages regarding sexuality. She has lived in the United States for four years. At high school, Sundara observes the American girls who are cheerleaders and is shocked by their conspicuous sexuality. The girls' behavior contrasts sharply with the strict customs and traditions in her family. When Sundara meets Jonathan, whom she likes very much, she becomes more aware of the diverse messages regarding sexuality. By gradually defining new relationships with others, she clarifies her own sexual identity and maintains appreciation for her cultural heritage.

In Childress' *Rainbow Jordan* (1981), the protagonist, Rainbow, also hears contradictory messages about sexuality from adults and peers. Rainbow stays with Miss Josephine, since her own mother has left home and only visits sporadically. When Rainbow begins to menstruate, Miss Josephine discusses sex with Rainbow and advises her to be very careful. Rainbow's mother is not a positive role model for healthy sexual relationships. Peers, both male and female, keep telling Rainbow that she is too standoffish for not being sexually active. This young woman becomes more adept at deciphering these messages as she gains pride and self-confidence. As a result, she becomes more intolerant of people who do not respect her.

Is Romance or Courtship Old-Fashioned Now?

Parents as well as adolescents perceive and can try to reconcile the cultural and generational differences in sexual attitudes and behaviors. A comparison between two novels, Maureen Daly's *Seventeenth Summer*, published in the 1940s, and Judy Blume's *Forever*, published in the 1970s, highlights the contrast between sexual practices of different eras.

Seventeenth Summer describes a slow courtship and romance between Angie Morrow and Jack Duluth during the three months of a summer. Angie's innocence and honesty make her different from the other girls whom Jack has dated. A cynical reader might anticipate that Jack would take advantage of Angie. He does not. They gradually develop companionship and more intimacy, even though there are misunderstandings along the way. Their sexual involvement consists primarily of holding and kissing. The author portrays the emotional intensity of sexual awakening with powerful depictions of the outdoors, family life, peer culture, and community norms. Eventually, Jack tells Angie that he has fallen in love with her. Their relationship ends at the close of summer with a gentle departure as Angie leaves for college. This novel does not overlook the pain of adolescence. Angie watches how her sister is dropped by a young man and she notes that nothing prepares us for all the "sadness in growing up" (203).

In *Forever*, a young woman named Katherine and her boyfriend, Michael, become sexually active in the context of a committed, caring relationship. This novel describes Katherine's first experience with intercourse and explores different aspects of teenagers' sexual decision making. Michael does not pressure Katherine to become sexually active until she is ready. Katherine also obtains information and birth control pills from Planned Parenthood. Although Michael and Katherine initially believe that their relationship is going to last forever, it does not. Katherine's feelings change while she is away from home at summer camp with her sister Jamie. As a reader, I was angered by Katherine's casual approach to the end of her relationship with Michael. This novel does not portray any of the same depth of character or feeling between two young people that is found in *Seventeenth Summer*.

Regardless of how much generations differ in attitudes toward sexual activity, adolescents face universal struggles. These two novels highlight how teenagers experience complex emotions while they deal with the psychological aspects of committed relationships. Both novels depict young people's first romance. There are similarities in the authors' descriptions of adolescents falling in love. These stories also describe how teens continually compare their own thinking to parents', peers', and siblings' input.

The Beautiful People

Look at how much physical attractiveness matters in our culture. Many people, young and old, strive to attain impossible standards of beauty promoted by magazines, television, and other media. Women who use these criteria to judge their own self-worth experience lowered self-esteem. Cultural definitions of thinness, beauty, and strength have been linked to the incidence of eating disorders, depression, and drug abuse.

Often, women become prisoners to societal messages. In Gary Paulsen's *Sisters* (1993), cultural myths of beauty and success snare two women. One is a prostitute, another is a cheerleader. At a dress shop, the cheerleader suddenly sees her own life mirrored in the prostitute's life. Although their worlds seem to differ, they are sisters, victims of society's standards. Each attempts to please others, outsmart the system, beat the odds, and fit images of success. These attempts only serve to move the women further into oppression.

Both males and females are preoccupied with the changes they experience during puberty. Female adolescents, however, are less satisfied with their physical appearance than males (Dacey and Kenny 1994, 91). Women's distorted body images surface in young adult fiction. In Alden Carter's *Up Country* (1989), Carl informs his girl-friend, Signa, that he always thought of her as being very confident of herself. Signa replies by saying: "But I've never felt sure of myself! And I don't like being built like a darn bulldozer. That night we made taffy, I went to bed thinking how much easier it'd be to get you if I looked more like Ginger or Debbie" (187).

Low self-esteem and cultural ideals of thinness often exacerbate negative perceptions of body image. In Lois Duncan's *Daughters of Eve* (1979), one of the young women, Laura, is overweight and insecure. Laura's mother asks her why she is so surprised that she has been invited into the exclusive Daughters of Eve Club. Laura thinks, "All [my] mother had to do was to look at [me], just once, with her eyes wide open. If she did, she might see [me] as [I] was, a 160-pound lump with a bust that looked like twin watermelons and a rear end that looked like twin something-elses" (13). Laura holds a Cinderella standard for seeing change and personal success in her own life:

> She wanted to belong to Daughters of Eve the way she wanted to look like Bambi Ellis—to be Homecoming Queen—to be cheerleader —to be able to lose twenty pounds overnight. She wanted it the way she wanted Peter Grange to fall in love with her. She wanted it the way, as a little girl, she had wanted to be a fairy princess so that she could wave her magic wand and mend all the cracks in her parents' splintering marriage. (14)

Similarly, the physical attractiveness of her peers provokes Carrie, the protagonist of Zibby Oneal's *The Language of Goldfish* (1980), to remark to herself, "Martha was another of the beautiful ones. She turned around and smiled at someone in the back of the room, reminding [me] of a girl in a Florida grapefruit commercial. They all reminded [me] of that, except for a few people" (18). These comparisons make Carrie feel like an outsider.

Bette Greene aptly describes how males respond adversely to cultural pressures about demonstrating masculinity through physical acts of aggression. In response to interview questions about her novel *The*

Drowning of Stephan Jones, Greene explains that men who love theatre, music, or books and who do not participate in sports at a young age can be victimized and ostracized in subcultures because of society's fear and hatred of homosexuality (Alvine 1994, 5–9).

The detrimental effects of unrealistic standards and peer pressures about sex on young men are illustrated in novels such as Judy Blume's *Forever* (1975). In this story, one young man who is very talented in theatre admits to a female friend that he is unsure about his own sexual identity. She tries to help him, but the crusade is misdirected. He needs time to find out who he is. Moreover, this young person feels unhappy and pressured because he does not have support at home for pursuing his interests in drama. We can see why his struggles are more difficult because he does not fit traditional models of masculinity. Eventually, this young man attempts suicide before obtaining professional help.

How I Look Is How I Feel

Both young adult fiction and psychological studies illustrate the reciprocal influence between individuals' psychological well-being and interpersonal attraction. This connection between our inner and outer world is illustrated in Lois Lowry's *A Summer to Die* (1977). The protagonist, Meg, always feels as if her sister is much more self-assured and beautiful than she is. Meg's perspective changes dramatically during the summer. She gains valuable experience and self-confidence, and with help from her family and new friendships, Meg copes bravely with her sister's illness and death. She also becomes aware of her own beauty. As her friend Will tells her, she has been beautiful all along. Meg just did not recognize it.

A similar change occurs in Cynthia Voigt's *Izzy, Willy-Nilly* (1986). After a painful recovery from a car accident, Izzy returns to school. No longer focusing exclusively on her outward appearance to feel healthy, Izzy recognizes how much she has changed when she sees one of her former friends, Lauren. Surrounded by boys, Lauren is beautiful. Yet, she seems unhappy and alone and wears a plastic smile. Izzy recognizes this sad, artificial pose and wonders why Lauren is pretending. Lauren, who does not have a nurturing family, relies solely on her physical attractiveness as a basis for self worth. The car accident forces Izzy to integrate her new physical self with a reformulated identity. With that change, she relies less on physical standards to judge her own loveliness.

Conclusion

People can become more realistic in their standards of beauty, intimacy, and attractiveness. Gaining experience with the emotional aspects of relationships provides one avenue for prompting such a shift. The universal struggles related to sexuality include maintaining one's own identity in intimate relationships, resisting peer pressure, developing moral codes, and integrating messages about sex from diverse sources. Resolving these issues strengthens the link between psychological well-being and interpersonal attraction, helping us to bypass unrealistic standards.

Works Cited

Alvine, L. 1994. "Understanding Adolescent Homophobia: An Interview with Bette Greene." *The Alan Review* 21(2): 5–9.

Banks, L. R. 1988. *Melusine: A Mystery*. New York: HarperKeypoint.

Blume, J. 1975. *Forever*. New York: Bradbury Press.

Bridgers, S. E. 1981. *Notes for Another Life*. New York: Bantam Books.

———. 1987. *Permanent Connections*. New York: HarperCollins.

Carter, A. 1989. *Up Country*. New York: Scholastic Inc.

Childress, A. 1981. *Rainbow Jordan*. New York: Avon Books.

Cormier, R. 1988. *Fade*. New York: Dell.

Crew, L. 1989. *Children of the River*. New York: Dell.

Crutcher, C. 1983. *Running Loose*. New York: Dell.

———. 1989. *Chinese Handcuffs*. New York: Dell.

Dacey, J., and M. Kenny. 1994. *Adolescent Development*. Madison, WI: WCB Brown & Benchmark.

Daly, M. 1942. *Seventeenth Summer*. New York: Pocket Books.

Duncan, L. 1979. *Daughters of Eve*. New York: Dell.

Erikson, E. 1968. *Identity: Youth & Crisis*. New York: W. W. Norton and Company.

Frank, A. 1995. *The Diary of a Young Girl: The Definitive Edition*. Translated by Susan Massotty. Edited by O. H. Frank and M. Pressler. New York: Doubleday.

Gilligan, C. 1988. "Remapping the Moral Domain: New Images of Self in Relationship." In *Mapping the Moral Domain: A Contribution of Women's Thinking to Psychological Theory and Education*, edited by C. Gilligan, J. V. Ward, J. M. Taylor, with B. Bardige, 3–19. Cambridge, MA: Harvard University Press.

Greene, B. 1991. *The Drowning of Stephan Jones*. New York: Bantam Books.

Hadley, L., and A. Irwin. 1985. *Abby, My Love*. New York: Atheneum Publishers.

Josselson, R. 1994. "Identity and Relatedness in the Life Cycle." In *Identity and Development: An Interdisciplinary Approach*, edited by H. A. Bosma, T. L. G. Graafsma, H. D. Grotevant, and D. J. de Levita, 81–101. Thousand Oaks, CA: Sage.

Kimmel, D. C., and I. Weiner. 1995. *Adolescence: A Developmental Transition.* 2d ed. New York: John Wiley & Sons.

Lerner, H. 1989. *The Dance of Intimacy: A Woman's Guide to Courageous Acts of Change in Key Relationships.* New York: Harper & Row.

Lowry, L. 1977. *A Summer to Die.* New York: Dell.

Oneal, Z. 1980. *The Language of Goldfish.* New York: Puffin Books.

Paterson, K. 1980. *Jacob Have I Loved.* New York: HarperKeypoint.

Paulsen, G. 1993. *Sisters.* San Diego: Harcourt, Brace & Company.

Pipher, M. 1994. *Reviving Ophelia: Saving the Selves of Adolescent Girls.* New York: Ballantine Books.

Sprinthall, N. A., and W. A. Collins. 1995. *Adolescent Psychology: A Developmental View.* New York: McGraw-Hill.

Steinberg, L. 1993. *Adolescence.* New York: McGraw-Hill.

Steinberg, L., and A. Levine. 1990. *You and Your Adolescent: A Parent's Guide For Ages Ten to Twenty.* New York: Harper & Row.

Voigt, C. 1986. *Izzy, Willy-Nilly.* New York: Aladdin Paperbacks.

Eight

I Must Be Going Crazy

*Sorrow may be fated, but to survive it and grow is an achievement
all its own.*

Robert Coles, *Children of Crisis*

Sometimes we press our noses against the window, longing to enter a
world that is different from the one we know. What is more admirable than having the will to grow, transform hardship, leave a prison
behind, and reenter the mainstream as newcomers to freedom? Yet
this spirit for change is easily outgrown or stifled. Many people living
in isolation, poverty, emotional illness, or even affluence and health
may never recognize any other way of life. We might not realize how
unusual or exceptional our own world is until we begin to talk with
others and have outside experiences. Teachers, parents, and others
have tremendous impact on adolescents' belief in their capacity for
self-improvement. The problems and growth of these adults can motivate young people to open their own worlds.

The film *The Shawshank Redemption*, about life at a prison,
describes how change can begin with a flicker of insight or a brief
glance at the outside world. In this movie, one convict, portrayed by
Morgan Freeman, knows that some people never leave the institute
because they are afraid and because confinement is the only world
they know. One man who finally departs from the jail eventually
commits suicide in the outside world. Yet another individual quietly
digs a tunnel out of the penitentiary and crawls to freedom without
anyone knowing about the escape until he is out. These outcomes and

other experiences move Morgan Freeman to eventually leave prison and become immersed in his own life of freedom.

Moving from any type of confinement to internal sources of pride and freedom is difficult for everyone, regardless of how troubled or healthy they are. Yet, this movement is a rich source of growth, self-respect, and compassion. Young people who cope with problems and survivors who recover can start from scratch, define themselves on new terms, bypass stereotypes, or find solutions of hope and courage against great odds.

We need to pay attention to these newcomers. Adolescents and others who overcome adversity can display a startling combination of innocence and hardship. Seeing the good even after difficult circumstances, they remain open to possibilities. Walking with the protagonists of young adult fiction, we trace their paths between pain and knowledge, risk and resiliency, illness and health. Our own black-and-white images of normal and abnormal begin to fade.

A Difficult Balancing Act

Unless we are describing the most extreme cases of disturbance, we encounter a gray area as we try to avoid exaggerating or minimizing the problems of young people. Striking a realistic balance between underestimating and overestimating adolescents' troubles is difficult.

Psychologists frequently refer to two broad categories of problems for adolescence. One category, labeled *externalizing disorders*, includes delinquency, running away, and problems of aggression. Overall, this set is more common among males and includes "undercontrolled" behaviors. The second category, labeled *internalizing disorders*, includes depression, anxiety, anorexia nervosa, and bulimia. This set, more common among women, refers to problems of internal distress. Adolescents can display problems in both of these broad categories concurrently (Steinberg 1993, 422–423; Sprinthall and Collins 1995, 406–408).

For many years, there were exaggerated claims about adolescence as a period of stress and turmoil (Elmen and Offer 1993, 5–7). Today, research indicates that the majority of parents and adolescents adjust relatively well to this stage of development. Psychologists caution against overstating adolescents' belief in their own invulnerability (Pipher 1994, 61) or underestimating their potential skill in judging risks (Quadrel et al. 1993, 102–116).

Nonetheless, adolescents are certainly vulnerable. Teenagers who are most in need of help are not receiving assistance (Elmen and Offer

1993, 16) or reach for the wrong kinds of help. Youth with nonsupportive relationships at home are more likely to become delinquent, join gangs, or use drugs in order to gain confidence and feel loved. Young teens can display distorted judgments, engage in risky experimentation, or show poor decision making skills. There is increased risk for the onset of disorders such as schizophrenia, anorexia nervosa, and bulimia during adolescence (Kimmel and Weiner 1995, 507, 533; Dacey and Kenny 1994, 361). Some adolescents hold romantic views of death, a factor linked to suicide in both psychology (Dacey and Kenny 1994, 375) and literature. Unrealistic concepts of death may stem partially from the media, teenagers' black-and-white thinking, and adolescents' egocentrism. These qualities are magnified in suicidal youth who are isolated and have poor coping skills.

It is easy to trivialize the problems of teenagers or underestimate the pressure on young people and their families today. In my classes, students voice genuine consternation about the increased stress and violence in their own lives. Concerns about school, losing a parent, and death are relatively common during early adolescence (Steinberg and Levine 1990, 157). Many teenagers can feel alone or overwhelmed as they cope with difficult situations. In class, students and guest lecturers provide examples of how adults dismiss young people's concerns with remarks such as "Oh, you're just going through a phase right now—it will pass" or "That's nothing. Just look at what our generation had to go through. What are you complaining about?"

The World Through Various Colored Glasses: Distorted Thinking

The majority of adolescents do not report exceptionally prolonged, internal strife. However, because teens experience so many changes simultaneously, they need guidance and reassurance as they sort through their feelings and cope with conflicts. Young adults can feel like outsiders and worry that they are not normal. Without a firm, stable identity, youths can have trouble separating confusion inside their head from the conflicting messages in the outside world. This lack of adequate sense of self can contribute to teenagers feeling like "It must be me. I'm the one who is going crazy."

The cultural milieu does not help. Society offers a steady stream of violence, crime, moral conflicts, and confusion. Yet, our media also presents glowing images of instant success, popularity, political correctness, and flashy idols. In *Reviving Ophelia: Saving the Selves of Adolescent Girls*, Mary Pipher (1994) defines our cultural bias for judging people solely on the basis of exterior qualities (23). In response, we devalue interior change as the source of freedom from our prisons. Moreover, the black-and-white images in our inner and outer worlds reflect society's mixed messages for adolescents. Our culture expects teenagers to grow up fast but does not offer them meaningful roles.

As Erik Erikson and other psychologists (Pipher 1994, 57–59) observe, it is no wonder that adolescents adopt extremes. Their extremism is not necessarily the tunnel vision of suicidal youth, but a typical response to cultural messages. Teens rely upon extremes in order to look normal to peers but abnormal to adults. These responses are often ways to avoid being subservient to others. Although temporary, extremes also mirror what mental health professionals label "distorted thinking." This term refers to thinking or doing the opposite of what will gain people more psychological strength. Overall, these extremes constrict individuals' freedom in their inner and outer worlds.

Diversions

Lack of information can lead us to overlook signs of disturbance in adolescents. Extremes of rebellion, self-criticism, conflict, or withdrawal, or dramatic changes in behavior are important indications of problems in youths. Ignoring these red flags can place adolescents and parents at peril. Yet we may miss these signs because young people can express symptoms in ways that differ from adults. For example, teens' restlessness, need for constant companionship, frenetic activity, and frequent complaints about boredom or fatigue may be manifestations of depression. Also, adolescents are less inclined to reveal their personal worries or admit their uncertainties because of where they are in their development (Cobb 1995, 571; Kimmel and Weiner 1995, 522).

The tendency to avoid talking about problems or to refuse to seek professional help surfaces in several young adult novels. In Fran Arrick's *Tunnel Vision* (1980), a father refuses to send his son to a counselor, insisting that his son will be able to resolve his problems without professional help. The father feels that if his son obtains counseling, it will indicate that he and his wife are not doing their job as parents. Not only the family but also friends and teachers view this boy's withdrawal, changes in physical appearances, drop in school performance, and preoccupation with death as a normal phase of adolescence.

In Richard Peck's *Remembering the Good Times* (1985), two friends, Buck and Kate, are profoundly affected by their friend Travis' suicide. Like others, they were unaware of how troubled he was. Travis was an excellent student yet always seemed very intense. Just before his death, he appeared calm and cheerful, but as Kate and Buck acknowledge later, Travis' poetry, conversations, and actions conveyed warnings.

They work hard to come to terms with this tragedy and seek more open communication as a prevention tool.

In Suzanne Newton's *I Will Call It Georgie's Blues* (1983), the Sloan family presents a polite, capable facade to the outside world. However, family members mask their true selves, which creates a stifling environment. When conflicts finally do surface, the facade begins to crumble. The youngest son, Georgie, repeatedly expresses his own distress signals. His withdrawal finally jolts the family away from deception and secrecy.

Family therapists are well aware that many times family members might focus on the "problem child" as a diversion from seeing their own unresolved issues or difficulties (Dacey and Kenny 1994, 221, 365; Minuchin and Nichols 1993, 36, 39). Judith Guest's *Ordinary People* (1976) is a moving portrayal of a family coping with the suicide attempt of one son and the death of another son. The father eventually recognizes how he ignores problems in his marriage by focusing exclusively on his sons' troubles. The relationship between the father and son improves, whereas the marital relationship becomes more strained. Eventually, the mother leaves home, resisting the family's healthy changes.

Silence about mental illness or family problems is often portrayed in young adult literature. In Zibby Oneal's *The Language of Goldfish* (1990), Carrie is reluctant to tell other people that she is seeing a psychiatrist. Oneal tells us:

> Then [Carrie] saw herself as someone else would see her—skinny and awkward and shy—a person who had to go day after day to a psychiatrist because she had cracked up in the fall.
> She was suddenly overwhelmed by this picture. How could she ever have considered telling people the truth? (131)

As Carrie recovers from a suicide attempt, she notices that her own mother never wants to talk about the attempt. "It would be better if they could talk about it, [Carrie] thought—so much better. It was as if there were a great ugly box in the middle of the room which everybody stepped around but would not admit was there" (Oneal 1990, 96). Although emotional illness, suicide, and other problems are very difficult, these issues need to be dealt with in a compassionate, caring way without blaming or criticizing.

Survival and Recovery

Survival and recovery are interrelated themes in young adult literature. Protagonists recover from their own suicide attempts (Conrad in Guest's *Ordinary People* and Carrie in Oneal's *The Language of Goldfish*);

mental illness (Deborah in Hannah Green's *I Never Promised You a Rose Garden*); the loss of a loved one through illness or death (Dillon in Chris Crutcher's *Chinese Handcuffs*; Louie in Chris Crutcher's *Running Loose*; the Tillerman children in Cynthia Voigt's *Homecoming* and *Dicey's Song*; and Bix in Bruce Brooks' *The Moves Make the Man*); alienation from family (Rob in Sue Ellen Bridgers' *Permanent Connections*), or a serious accident (Izzy in Cynthia Voigt's *Izzy, Willy-Nilly*).

Survivors who recover from a loss or illness, and other people who surmount problems, can develop new inner resources. Their most significant changes occur gradually and replace loss of hope or bitter disillusionment. Gaining new purpose and poise despite hardship, they also have a more realistic perspective on themselves and recognize the unsuccessful coping skills they used in the past.

For some, the process of recovery resembles climbing slowly from the bottom of a barrel. In Green's *I Never Promised You a Rose Garden* (1991), Deborah recovers from mental illness with the help of a dedicated doctor. She recognizes one day that she is going to live:

> Slowly and steadily, Deborah began to see the colors in the world. She saw the form and the colors of the trees and the walkway and the hedge and over the hedge to the winter sky. The sun went down and the tones began to vibrate in the twilight. . . . And in a slow, oncoming way, widening from a beginning, it appeared to Deborah that she would not die. It came upon her with a steady, mounting clarity that she was going to be more than undead, that she was going to be alive. It had a sense of wonder and awe, great joy and trepidation. (192)

For Deborah, this shift from illness to health is long, slow, and frightening. Her progress resembles the prisoner in the film *The Shawshank Redemption* who escapes prison by digging a tunnel, inch by inch, with a small tool. There is no fanfare while he works. However, others express amazement after he escapes. As people became aware of Deborah's effort, they can recognize how extraordinary her recovery is.

Young adult literature accurately depicts the struggles of families of the emotionally ill. Examples include Voigt's *Homecoming* (1981), Bridgers' *Notes for Another Life* (1981), and *I Never Promised You a Rose Garden* (1964). These individuals face unusual stress as they cope with the chronic illness of a person they love. In her book *The Hidden Victims*, Julie Tallard Johnson (1988), a psychotherapist, examines the complex issues that families of the mentally ill face. As Johnson emphasizes, these families face a difficult balancing act of caring for the mentally ill person and managing their own lives. Every individual is affected. Some people may try to escape or become detached, while others may assume too much responsibility for the care of the ill person. The families may also isolate themselves and refuse to discuss the mental illness.

The love and work that inspire hope and change in families is beautifully illustrated in novels such as Bridgers' *Notes for Another Life* (1981). A brother and a sister bravely cope with the mental illness of their father, who is hospitalized. The sister, Wren, voices her own realization that she can take nothing for granted. While she is with her boyfriend Sam, she wonders:

> How can he be so sure of everything . . . when he's just a year older than me? Hasn't he ever felt his confidence snagged against experience like I have? You couldn't have a father in and out of mental hospitals without wondering about yourself. (57)

Her brother, Kevin, assists and cares more for his father as he addresses his own problems, gains emotional autonomy, and establishes healthier connections to others.

People who are recovering from illness or trauma also cope with the reactions of other individuals. They may feel like family and friends initially treat them with kid gloves. Some go out of their way to be careful not to do anything that might upset family or friends. Deborah of *I Never Promised You a Rose Garden* knew this feeling all too well when she first visited her family after a lengthy stay in the hospital ward. Carrie in *The Language of Goldfish* and Conrad of *Ordinary People* notice this special treatment when they first return from the hospital. More than anything, these survivors crave being treated like everyone else. Over time, others become less overprotective or careful. In *The Language of Goldfish*, Carrie welcomes this shift:

> Once in a while she recognized that there had been small changes since Christmas. Three months ago Sophie would have spoken to her carefully about her book bag if she'd mentioned it at all. Today, she could just as well have been yelling at Duncan. (Oneal 1990, 124)

Peers at school tease or brand them as different, yet these protagonists respond by reaching a core anger that motivates change. In *The Language of Goldfish*, Carrie's outrage at a classmate's insult makes her plunge more into the mainstream of life and become stronger. In *Ordinary People*, Conrad, recovering from a suicide attempt, is offended by another young man's taunt and becomes involved in a fight. This confrontation shows his reimmersion in life.

Other survivors in young adult literature learn to educate and inspire others through their actions. Anne Frank is the antithesis of whatever maladjustment could develop in people who face extreme adversity. Despite living in such deprived conditions, Anne displays remarkable strength. She survives as a person who remains open to possibilities, shows a desire to grow, and expresses her willingness to trust in good things. Anne is not out of touch with reality. Her diary contains realistic accounts of many difficulties that she and her family experience. They know what is happening to other Jewish people in the concentration camps, and they obtain information about the war through contacts. Although events occur that are beyond Anne's control, she matures and surpasses many people who live in more fortunate circumstances.

Young adult fiction accurately portrays how adolescents and adults who face difficulties may not cope well or survive. In Guest's *Ordinary People* (1976), a young woman who stayed at the same hospital as Conrad commits suicide. In Green's *I Never Promised You a Rose Garden* (1964), Deborah realizes that many patients will never leave the hospital ward. Others function in the outside world in spite of their troubles while some are "numb" to their troubles, retreating into denial.

There are examples in young adult literature of survivors who, despite their endurance, initially use strategies to seal off harsh truths and compartmentalize these events from other aspects of their lives. Some may focus on a dream in order to survive. At one time, they may not be able to deal with painful circumstances but are able to function well in other areas. Perhaps these protective maneuvers stem partially from the inability to come to terms with the reality that bad things happen to good people. This dynamic provides some protagonists of young adult literature with temporary focus, endurance, or elaborate game plans. Later, they realize what they did at an earlier time in order to survive or cope. They gradually become better able to integrate the different components of their lives.

The change in perspective is illustrated in Alden Carter's *Up Country* (1989). In this novel, the protagonist, Carl, copes with a chaotic lifestyle while living with his alcoholic mother. When his mother is arrested, Carl is temporarily moved from his home to live with relatives. Here, he meets new people who are warm and caring. This environment offers stability. With guidance from family, friends, and counselors, Carl begins to recognize and work on his own problems as the son of an alcoholic.

Carl eventually looks back at his former lifestyle and realizes what he has done for years in order to survive: "I just wandered off into a dreamworld. I moved to the basement and started getting really heavy into electronics" (229). Carl used to fantasize about a calm dream life with an imaginary woman named Jennifer as an escape. Eventually, reality infiltrates his dreams and replaces this fantasy. Carl does not realize how much his own life has been affected by his mother's alcoholism until later, when he is in a more stable environment.

Like Carl, other protagonists make important discoveries about themselves and recognize that the outside world differs from their prior expectations. They become more realistic in their appraisals of self and others. A confrontation, loss, or accident prompts several young people to face their problems. Adolescents' new knowledge about signs of trouble and health also sharpens understanding that the oddball may be a champion of freedom rather than a victim of oppression and that people who look well-adjusted may be very troubled. Like a peephole of light, this dawning awareness is an entrance to emotional freedom.

Integration

The insights and experiences mentioned in the previous section enable people to gradually reverse their distorted thinking and move toward psychological strength. The protagonists of young adult literature often learn by confronting the most disturbing images and fears inside their heads and hearts. Internally, they discover solutions in the last place they expected. Innocence, frailty, suffering, and illness can inspire wisdom, beauty, strength, and health. In fiction, people's ability to unify these divergent experiences parallels Erik Erikson's, Harriet Lerner's, and other psychologists' emphasis on integrating rather than polarizing opposites.

Blending dichotomies, literature and psychology can teach us to juxtapose normal and abnormal. This is illustrated by the provocative opening statement of Susanna Kaysen's book *Girl, Interrupted* (1993) as she describes her stay as a teenager on a psychiatric ward:

> People ask, How did you get in there? What they really want to know is if they are likely to end up in there as well. I can't answer the real question. All I can tell them is, It's easy. (5)

Acknowledging our vulnerabilities can be a source of freedom, reflecting the gray area between illness and health. As Dillon Hemingway of Crutcher's *Chinese Handcuffs* (1989) says "I can't look at the horror in anyone without looking at the horror in myself" (15). Instead of confining us, this link enriches our inner and outer world. It also helps debunk the myth that "I'm the one with a weird family. Everybody else's family is normal."

Integration evolves continuously as adolescents and adults negotiate many of the developmental issues described in this text. Young adult literature and psychology underline the ongoing synthesis of opposing tensions. Identity, individuation, and autonomy evolve in the context of close relationships rather than through detachment. People move closer to becoming the persons they want to be by dropping fronts in close relationships. Resolving conflicts inside the head enables us to accomplish realistic action in the outside world. Young adult literature and psychological studies show how coping with setbacks, defeat, and problems can be important sources of pride and achievement rather than shame. Individuals may develop courage in the context of fear and relinquish black-and-white definitions of truth or authority as they face moral dilemmas. Instead of splitting the bad from the good, adolescents and adults can cultivate healthy perspectives on their sexuality by consolidating its different components. Finally, connections between abnormal and normal provide another source of freedom.

Conclusion

Merging young adult fiction and adolescent psychology can help teachers and parents to gain more accurate knowledge about teenagers' problems and vulnerabilities. Both genres offer balance between underestimating and overestimating the disorders of adolescence. Survivors and others who cope successfully with difficulties can realistically appraise painful truths, still trust in good things, remain open to new possibilities, and seek change. The integration of freedom and compassion allows us to find our own mix of innocence and hardship as we tackle difficult problems.

Works Cited

Arrick, F. 1980. *Tunnel Vision.* Scarsdale: Bradbury Press.

Bridgers, S. E. 1981. *Notes for Another Life.* New York: Bantam Books.

———. 1987. *Permanent Connections.* New York: HarperKeypoint.

Brooks, B. 1984. *The Moves Make the Man.* New York: HarperKeypoint.

Carter, A. 1989. *Up Country.* New York: Scholastic.

Cobb, N. J. 1995. *Adolescence: Continuity, Change and Diversity.* Mountain View, CA: Mayfield.

Coles, R. 1967. *Children of Crisis: A Study of Courage and Fear.* Boston: Little, Brown & Company.

Crutcher, C. 1983. *Running Loose.* New York: Dell.

———. 1989. *Chinese Handcuffs.* New York: Dell.

Dacey, J., and M. Kenny. 1994. *Adolescent Development.* Madison, WI: WCB Brown & Benchmark.

Elmen, J., and D. Offer. 1993. "Normality, Turmoil, and Adolescence." In *Handbook of Clinical Research and Practice with Adolescents,* edited by P. Tolan and B. J. Cohler, 5–19. New York: John Wiley & Sons.

Erikson, E. 1968. *Identity: Youth and Crisis.* New York: W. W. Norton & Company.

Frank, A. 1995. *The Diary of a Young Girl: The Definitive Edition*. Translated by Susan Massotty. Edited by O. H. Frank and M. Pressler. New York: Doubleday.

Green, H. 1964. *I Never Promised You a Rose Garden*. New York: Holt, Rinehart & Winston.

Guest, J. 1976. *Ordinary People*. New York: Ballantine Books.

Johnson, J. T. 1988. *Hidden Victims: An Eight-Stage Healing Process for Families and Friends of the Mentally Ill*. New York: Doubleday.

Kaysen, S. 1993. *Girl, Interrupted*. New York: Turtle Bay Books.

Kimmel, D. C., and I. Weiner. 1995. *Adolescence: A Developmental Transition*. 2d ed. New York: John Wiley & Sons.

Lerner, H. 1985. *The Dance of Anger: A Woman's Guide to Changing the Patterns of Intimate Relationships*. New York: Harper & Row.

Minuchin, S., and M. P. Nichols. 1993. *Family Healing: Strategies for Hope and Understanding*. New York: Simon & Schuster.

Newton, S. 1983. *I Will Call It Georgie's Blues*. New York: Puffin Books.

Oneal, Z. 1990. *The Language of Goldfish*. New York: Puffin Books.

Paterson, K. 1978. *The Great Gilly Hopkins*. New York: HarperCollins.

Peck, R. 1985. *Remembering the Good Times*. New York: Dell.

Pipher, M. 1994. *Reviving Ophelia: Saving the Selves of Adolescent Girls*. New York: Ballantine Books.

Quadrel, M. J., B. Fischhoff, and W. Davis. 1993. "Adolescent (In)vulnerability." *American Psychologist* 48(2): 102–16.

The Shawshank Redemption. 1995. Directed by Frank Darabont. 142 minutes. TriStar Films. Videocassette.

Sprinthall, N. A., and W. A. Collins. 1995. *Adolescent Psychology: A Developmental View*. New York: McGraw-Hill.

Steinberg, L. 1993. *Adolescence*. 3d. ed. New York: McGraw-Hill.

Steinberg, L., and A. Levine. 1990. *You and Your Adolescent: A Parent's Guide for Ages Ten to Twenty*. New York: Harper & Row.

Voigt, C. 1981. *Homecoming*. New York: Ballantine Books.

———. 1982. *Dicey's Song*. New York: Ballantine Books.

———. 1986. *Izzy, Willy-Nilly*. New York: Aladdin Paperbacks.